# GIANT STEPS

*A true story from
Africa about exploitation
and the meaning of freedom*

## Richard Peirce

Principal photographers Jacqui and Richard Peirce

Struik Nature
(an imprint of Penguin Random House South Africa (Pty) Ltd)
Reg. No. 1953/000441/07
The Estuaries No. 4, Oxbow Crescent (off Century Avenue),
Century City, 7441 South Africa
PO Box 1144, Cape Town, 8000 South Africa

Visit www.randomstruik.co.za and join the Struik Nature Club
for updates, news, events and special offers.

First published in 2016
10 9 8 7 6 5 4 3 2 1

Publisher: Pippa Parker
Editor: Helen de Villiers
Designer: Janice Evans
Reproduction by Hirt & Carter Cape (Pty) Ltd
Printed and bound by DJE Flexible Print Solutions

Print: 978-1-77584-330-6
epub: 978-1-77584-331-3
ePDF: 978-1-77584-332-0

Textured background: Elephant poop paper by Thaily-stock

## PICTURE CREDITS

Heinrich van den Berg: front cover
Bradley Jonathan Sheldon: back cover top
AF Archive/Alamy/Afripics: p.64
Jenny Brooker: pp.7, 44, 50-51, 54 (both), 56-57,
69, 70-71, 96, 99 (all), 102-103 (all), 109
Colour Library/Images of Africa: p.168
The David Sheldrick Wildlife Trust.
www.iworry.org: p.166

Roger de la Harpe/Images of Africa: p.158
Nigel Dennis/Images of Africa: p.15
ITV/Rex Shutterstock: p.58
Gerhard Steenkamp: pp.72, 75, 76-77, 78 bottom,
79, 80-81 (all), 82 (both), 84 (both)
Roger Titley: p.60
Hein von Hörsten/Images of Africa: pp.163-164,
172-173
WNET: p.167

## DEDICATION

This book is dedicated to all those who work trying to ensure a wild future for
Africa's animals. It is also to say thank you to Ronnie Wood who is only rarely
recognised for his contributions to wildlife conservation.

*Part of the sale proceeds from* Giant Steps *will support the work of Tusk. However, the
content of* Giant Steps *is entirely mine and does not necessarily reflect views held by Tusk.*

# CONTENTS

# FOREWORDS

Apart from the day-to-day challenges of living in the wild, the main problem elephants face is that they share the planet with an ever-increasing, greedy, and out of control human race.

Physically, humans are nothing like elephants; however, mentally, we resemble each other closely. Elephants show affection, mourn their dead, communicate using a large vocabulary, possess long memories, have highly developed brains, and live in groups with defined social structures.

Doubtless elephants will survive as exhibits in zoos and game parks, but it remains to be seen whether we will allow them the space to continue to live as truly wild animals. At the moment the demand from China and south-east Asia for ivory and other wildlife products seems insatiable. Nevertheless, every wildlife campaigner hopes this demand can be reduced and reversed. What seems impossible to reverse is human population expansion.

In the end, the question will probably be, is the planet big enough for both humans and wild elephants?

On today's evidence the answer is likely to be no. It will be a terrible tragedy if this magnificent and intelligent animal is reduced to being peered at as a curiosity in zoos and game parks.

Jacqui Peirce

*Giant Steps* is the true story of two African elephants – Bully and Induna. Both elephants were orphans, and one has been much luckier in his life than the other.

Their story involves happiness and sadness, cruelty, deprivation, and the loss of their natural lives. Researching *Giant Steps* brought me face to face with some awkward questions; in days gone by when elephants were culled, was it right to spare the babies? Is it ever defensible to train such intelligent animals and keep them in captivity? Should elephants be kept in captivity at all? Will ivory poaching be stopped before elephants, and many other animals, become extinct in the wild?

I have tried to use the story of Bully and Induna to ask pertinent questions and look for answers. Researching their life stories has involved an extraordinary journey, which has reinforced to me what amazing animals elephants are; to think of one elephant being killed every 15–20 minutes by poachers doesn't just send a shiver down my spine, it makes me very angry. The picture of Bully or Induna lying dead with their head in a pool of blood, and with their tusks hacked out is the stuff of nightmares; and the nightmare is happening at the rate of nearly 100 elephants a day.

Africa without its wildlife wouldn't be Africa as the world knows it. I hope that humans can follow in Bully and Induna's giant steps, and win the struggle to conserve Africa's remaining wildlife before it has disappeared forever from the continent's wild places.

Richard Pierce

# ACKNOWLEDGEMENTS

When researching this book it was a pleasure and a privilege to retrace Bully and Induna's 'Giant Steps'. Along the way I have received an enormous amount of help from many people; I would like to thank the following for their help, and apologise to anyone I have inadvertently left out.

Anne Albert; Lawrence Anthony (author of *The Elephant Whisperer*); John, Jenny and Jonathan Brooker; Dan Bucknell; James Clarke (author of *Save Me from the Lion's Mouth*); Trevor Carnaby (author of *Beat about the Bush*); Brenda du Toit, Denise Headon & Madelein Marais for their research and for making up for my keyboard ineptitude; Inverdoorn Game Reserve – Jean-Michel, Cathie & Damian Vergnaud, Christo and all the rangers at the Reserve; Lindie and Sean Hensman; Candice Luddick; Dalene Matthee (author of *Circles in the Forest*); Charles Mayhew MBE; Nigel Morgan; Knysna Elephant Park; Mishak Mbaur; NSPCA; Louis Olivier; Wilna Paxton; Mitch Reardon (author of *Shaping Kruger*); Dame Daphne Sheldrick (author of *African Love Story*); Wilbur Smith; Dr Jo Shaw; Dr Gerhard Steenkamp; Will Travers OBE; Karen Trendler; Tusk; Sias van Rooyan; The Windsor Hotel (Hermanus); Lyall Watson (author of *Elephantoms*); Lisette Withers; Dr Debbie Young; Nick Muller, director of Dispute Resolution at Cliffe Dekker Hofmeyr, for his invaluable advice; and all those at my publishers Struik Nature – Pippa Parker, Helen de Villiers, Janice Evans and Belinda van der Merwe – firstly for doing such a brilliant job putting this book together, and secondly for having the patience to deal with what I am sure must be one of their more troublesome authors!

Finally, a zillion thanks to my wife Jacqui who takes most of the photos, remembers to bring the voice recorders, asks the questions I have forgotten, and doesn't throw something at my head when she is told to shush (for the twentieth time that day).

# AFRICAN ELEPHANT FACTS

- The visible part of an elephant's tusk is about two-thirds of its total length.
- Tusks grow fastest between an elephant's 35th and 40th year.
- In most four-legged species the female's teats are found between the hind legs; unusually, an elephant's teats are between her front legs.
- Male elephants have no scrotum. Their testes are located internally near their kidneys.
- Bull elephants ejaculate 1.5 litres (a third of a gallon) of semen.
- Elephants have 28 teeth in their lives, including two milk tusks that often don't show, and are replaced by permanent tusks, which continue growing for most of their lives.
- Tusks are actually upper incisor teeth.
- Elephants don't have four knees. Their front 'knees' are, in fact, wrists.
- Elephants trumpet by forcing air through their trunk so violently that the nasal mucosa and septum resonate, and these sounds are amplified by the trunk's long tunnels (nostrils).
- Trunks have about 150,000 muscles and no bones, making them very flexible.
- The gestation period is 22 months (the longest of any land animal), and the nursing period can be up to five years.
- Each day African elephants drink about 230 litres (50 gallons) of water, and consume up to 180 kilograms (400 pounds) of food.

- An elephant sleeps for only two to four hours each day.
- At any one time elephants can hold some 18 litres (4 gallons) or more of water in their trunk.
- Elephants have poor eyesight and only see clearly up to a distance of about 18 metres (60 feet).
- An adult African elephant's brain weighs 4.5 kilograms (10 pounds).
- Elephant cows usually weigh about 4 tonnes and bulls up to 6 tonnes.
- Their large, floppy ears do more than hear. With lots of tiny veins transecting the surface, and carrying cooled blood to the rest of the body, their ears act as a cooling system. Ear flapping can also be used to get rid of insects or to indicate anger.
- The average elephant lifespan in the wild is 60 to 70 years.
- That elephants set up 'graveyards' is a myth, but they do recognise the bones/skeletal remains of relatives.
- Tusks are used for defence and fighting among bulls, and for collecting food items.
- There are two main elephant species: the African and the Asian, and there is ongoing debate as to whether the African forest elephant is a separate species.
- When Hannibal invaded Europe in 218BC, he used elephants to help carry his army and its equipment across the Alps.
- Elephants are the only animal with large round or oval tracks. Asian elephants have five toenails on the front feet and four on the back, while African bush elephants have four on the front and three on the back. African forest elephants have the same number of toenails as Asian elephants.

# PART ONE

The golden orb
made its fiery
appearance.

# 1

# THE KRUGER NATIONAL PARK

The bull elephant appeared to know exactly where the sun would appear over the faraway hills in the Tankwa Karoo. He raised his trunk, seeming to salute the birth of a new day, and pointing at the precise spot where, moments later, the golden orb would make its fiery appearance.

He sniffed the air as if savouring his freedom. Behind him the younger bull was intent on denuding a small tree of its foliage. The two elephants, Bully and Induna, had come a long way on their journey to safety and freedom.

In the back of Bully's mind were nearly forgotten memories of his mother's panic, of loss and sadness, and of deprivation, fear and uncertainty. Bully's mother had been his group's matriarch and had been the first to go down when his family were culled all around him in the Kruger National Park in 1992.

Ninety years earlier, in July 1902, Major James Stevenson-Hamilton had been appointed as the first warden of the new Sabie Game Reserve. The Park's headquarters were at Sabie Bridge, now known as Skukuza. In May 1926 the National Parks Act was passed, and the Sabie and Shingwedzi game reserves were merged to form the Kruger National Park.

The Park is 380 kilometres long and, on average, 60 kilometres wide. At approximately 20,000 square kilometres, it is larger than many small countries. It is thought to be home to about 50 percent of South Africa's insect diversity, has 505 bird species, 118 reptiles, 35 amphibians, 50 indigenous 'water' species, and 148 mammals. The Park also supports a diversity of approximately 2,000 plant species.

Despite the Kruger's size and biodiversity, it is a limited area with hard boundaries; as a result, scientists and Park wardens have had to manage species according to the area's ability to support them. This ability of an area to support one species or another is often referred to as its carrying capacity.

It used to be thought that the Kruger Park's elephant-carrying capacity was approximately 7,000 animals, which is roughly one elephant per 2.6 square kilometres (1 square mile). The natural ability of the land to sustain elephant numbers was progressively altered by the construction of numerous watering holes, many of which have now been removed. In 1967 the first aerial survey of the Park estimated an elephant population of 6,500.

Annual culls started as a management tool to ensure that the Park's elephant-carrying capacity was maintained at what was considered to be a sustainable level. By the time culling was stopped in 1994, over 16,000 elephants had been killed. Later, in 2005, the increasing elephant population caused South African National Parks (SANParks) to once again consider culling as a means of management. The resulting global outcry forced any further consideration of this option to be abandoned.

The sheer size of the Earth's largest land mammals makes them difficult to manage and live with due to the huge volume of food they require, and the land area needed to provide this amount of material. Elephants are massive consumers: they forage for up to 20 hours a day and eat up to 50 tonnes of vegetation each year – a formidable impact on the environment. However, they are not simply a destructive force as they also provide valuable services to their surroundings, such as seed dispersal, opening up thickets and facilitating the development of areas of grazing grasses for other species.

When Bully was born the culling policy was still in force and his was among the last families to be wiped out. Helicopters, dart guns, large-calibre rifles and pistols all had their place as the tools of elephant destruction. Pilots and rangers worked together to kill as quickly and efficiently as possible, having perfected their techniques over time.

Elephants forage for up to 20 hours a day and eat about 50 tonnes of vegetation each year.

After 22 months of pregnancy Bully's was a trouble-free birth. His mother was the family group's matriarch and Bully was her sixth calf. She had left the group a few days earlier, accompanied by her younger sister, and late one afternoon – knowing her time had come – she chose a clean, flat, sandy area and squatted to begin her labour. First there was a huge gush of fluid, then she strained and Bully's head appeared. She adjusted her position slightly, gave a massive heave and Bully dropped to the ground, a wet-looking jumble of fluid, purplish foetal sac, mucous-coated membrane, and baby elephant.

The little calf lay still as his mother stripped away the membrane with the tip of her trunk. The umbilical cord had broken as he fell and the calf lay still, as if dead. His mother gave him a gentle shove with her foot and rolled him slightly. Immediately, and as if in protest at being disturbed, he began to kick violently. His mother caressed him with her trunk and carefully lifted him to his feet. He fell over immediately, then got up by himself, wobbled, and raised his little trunk. An experienced mother, she next guided the calf to the two teats between her front legs and soon he was feeding contentedly.

A few days later they rejoined the herd and, one by one, the other elephants came to inspect and acquaint themselves with the new arrival. There were two other recently borne calves, both were female, and they came together to greet the new baby.

His father didn't spend much time with the group. He reappeared when females were in oestrus but otherwise was content with his own company or that of other males. He would often spend weeks with his bachelor group, then wander off again on an apparently endless quest. In his early 40s and fully mature, he was one of the largest bulls in the Park, standing over 4 metres (13 feet) at the shoulder and weighing well over 6 tonnes. He was a majestic and awe-inspiring sight as he made his stately way around his domain.

He would sometimes seek high ground and stare into the distance for long periods of time, usually facing to the north. Elephants do not have good eyesight, but he was 'seeing' with his brain, rather than with his eyes. His mind struggled with memories. He had been born across the Limpopo River, and in a drought many years ago his herd had crossed the river, heading south looking for food sources to support their huge needs. As he stared into the distance it was as if he were remembering yesterday's Africa, a land of fewer fences, fewer people, fewer guns and, for elephants, fewer challenges, threats or stresses.

Bully's mother was a large cow and she complemented his father's size, standing over 3 metres (10 feet) at the shoulder. If the gene mix ran true, Bully would eventually be a very large bull himself. He was cheeky, playful, precocious and a baby, all at once. From the moment they are born baby elephants start being educated by their elders. Bully was learning the rules fast, but was quick to return to his mother for protection as soon as he felt threatened or insecure.

He was good at falling over things and getting his legs tangled up. His mother and the other older elephants would often pause in their endless feeding to watch the baby clown getting up to his antics. With an amused, tolerant and affectionate air his mother would watch her son chase after an older baby calf, misjudge an obstacle on the ground, and end up in an undignified heap of trunk, legs and ears.

Bully's was an idyllic, happy world, but it was about to be shattered, and his life would change forever. There were 14 elephants in Bully's family group, and this was an ideal number of animals to take out in a cull.

Playing and fun was soon
to be replaced by a new world
of panic and darkness.

# 2

# GREY CLOUDS GATHER

John Brooker is a South African of English origin whose life has been closely entwined with that of wild animals. Since the 1960s he has worked all over Africa, involved in the live capture of dangerous, rare and threatened species. To many people, men like Brooker are contradictions; hunters who are conservationists, animal capturers who are trying to save wildlife. However, a closer examination of the facts and the motives behind their actions dispels the contradictions, and reveals that men like Brooker are at least partly responsible for several successful conservation initiatives.

In 1969 Brooker started making a film called 'A Case for Survival', which not only showed his love for African wildlife, it also proved him to be a man ahead of his time. The film's English narration now sounds dated and stilted, and production values are lower than they would have been had the film been made today. Nevertheless, the message is clear and shows that Brooker had a sophisticated grasp of conservation issues over 40 years ago, when many still had their heads in the sand.

Early in 1991 John Brooker was contacted by SANParks and asked if he would try and rear baby elephants that had become orphans as a result of culling. As milk calves, they were wholly reliant on their mothers. Some weaned infants were able to be sold into captivity, but foster parents would have to be found for the milk babies or they would have to be culled along with the rest of the herd. Many attempts had been made to hand-rear elephant milk calves. Daphne Sheldrick in Kenya, Rory Hensman in Zimbabwe and others had enjoyed varying degrees of success, but as far as Brooker was aware, no 100 percent-successful formula had been found.

He realised that, in some ways, he was being placed in a no-win position. If he failed the calves would die, and if he succeeded he might be condemning them to a life in captivity with uncertain futures. Certainly they would become heavily habituated to humans, and quite possibly would never return to knowing freedom in the wild and living as elephants should. On a strictly pragmatic level he knew he probably should leave the babies to be killed with their herd. But he was a fighter who loved a challenge and something told him he could do it. What's more, he was also compassionate and believed in saving life if he could.

'Old Joe' was from the Pedi tribe and no-one knew exactly how old he was (he had few teeth and very little hair); he was probably younger than his name suggested but the name suited him so 'Old Joe' he was to everyone. He had worked for John Brooker since 1972 and was John's right-hand man. As an animal handler he possessed extraordinary ability. Whether with elephants or lions he was fearless, and he had silent ways of communicating with animals. Visually Old Joe was not immediately an impressive character, but he radiated a cheerful, honest, calm happiness that was recognised by both humans and animals.

Successfully rearing baby elephant milk calves would require luck, judgement, experimentation and intuition. Old Joe's intuitive ways with animals would be of huge value rearing the orphaned baby elephants.

Taking on traumatised, hungry, frightened baby elephants, and not having a fully successful milk product on which to rear them was a daunting prospect that would have put off even experienced operators. John and Old Joe approached it with calm confidence.

In early May 1992 John woke to a clear, bright and sunny day, but couldn't dispel the dark clouds in the back of his mind. Culling was underway in the Kruger Park; he was no stranger to culls, having often witnessed them and even taken part in them. Now he was standing by to take away any of the tiny milk calves that were spared.

Culls were kind on neither the eye nor the ear, and, in John's case, every cull was now more difficult to deal with mentally than the one before had been.

Man is naturally a hunter and, no matter how urbanised or civilised we become, our primeval instincts are not very deeply buried. Just as going to war produces an emotional mixture of dread and excitement, so did the prospect of a cull. As John began his day, a cocktail of emotions and thoughts fizzed in his brain: revulsion, because he knew what was coming; elation at the thought of saving calves; and adrenalin-fuelled excitement. By the end of the day it was likely he would be a surrogate parent to several orphans.

Just before midday he received a message telling him that a suitable group of elephants had been identified near the Crocodile River Road west of Crocodile Bridge and east of Malelane. He was to prepare his vehicle and standby to proceed in convoy to the cull site. John went to find Old Joe to give him the news, and tell him to start getting things ready. A heavy sadness hung between the two men as John told Old Joe there would be orphans today.

Bully's mother and the rest of the group were awake and browsing long before first light. A baby, two other milk calves, three youngsters and eight adults browsing and grazing make many different noises. A major responsibility of the matriarch is keeping the herd safe, and

Bully's mother's brain separated out each sound and analysed it; if it promised no threat, she stored it away and was happy.

Unless Bully was more careful, however, he would come a cropper. He had just finished playing with the young six-year-old bull and his game had proved too annoying, so he had received a hefty slap. His immediate elders were tolerant of the new baby, but tolerance only went so far, and Bully hadn't yet learned how to tell where too far was. He ran squealing for the safety zone between his mother's two front legs, but it didn't take long for his confidence to return, and for him to venture out and back to play. He had almost forgotten his recent rebuke and his play would soon incur another reprimand.

Two or three hours after dawn, his mother's acute hearing picked up the distant hum of an aircraft – a helicopter. She turned her head in the direction of the noise but this was more an orientation move than an expectation of seeing anything as elephants have very poor eyesight. The sound was still a long way off so she carried on browsing, but she soon detected it was coming closer and instinct warned her of danger. Her younger sister picked up her disquiet and together they changed direction and started to lead the herd away from the approaching noise.

The machine arrived overhead but stayed quite high, and the pilot hovered while the spotter radioed a description of the herd back to ranger H.Q. at Skukuza. Fourteen animals was an appropriately sized group and they were in an area that was easy to seal off from the prying, and probably disapproving, eyes of Park visitors.

The decision to cull the group was made and the pilot was ordered to leave the area to avoid spooking the animals. The word was passed to John and others to prepare and stand by to move to the cull site.

By late morning the recovery team convoy had assembled and was ready to leave Skukuza. Three large trucks, a smaller truck with a hydraulic loading arm, three Land Rovers with rangers and butchers, and John Brooker's vehicle were all ready to go.

One of the factors taken into consideration when deciding which animals to cull, and where, was their tendency to leave the Park and damage crops and property in adjacent areas. On the other side of the Crocodile River is rich farmland where sugar cane and citrus fruits are grown. These crops are favourites of elephants.

The huge damage caused to crops was reason enough for farmers to shoot them. Very often the calibre of rifle used was too light, or the shooting not accurate enough, and elephants with serious gunshot wounds were common. Both to protect crops and to avoid wounding of animals, herds close to exit and entry areas were often cleared by culling.

Bully's family herd were browsing very close to the river and had placed themselves in a zone of maximum danger. They were in the wrong place at the wrong time.

The Crocodile River road and other access points were closed to avoid any Park visitors witnessing the horror of the cull, as SANParks were understandably very sensitive to public opinion. What was about to happen would turn the strongest stomach and cause massive distress if seen by visitors. There are two sides to every coin: from SANParks' perspective, they were carrying out a distasteful but necessary management measure for the benefit of the Park in general, as well as for the remaining elephants; whereas Park visitors would regard the cull as being of the utmost cruelty and barbarity, and would have little sympathy for the rangers who were simply doing their job. The two opposing viewpoints were irreconcilable. For this reason SANParks tried to conduct culls as fast and efficiently as possible to minimise stress and suffering for the elephants, and to avoid inviting public criticism. The age-old adage that elephants have long memories is correct, as is the newer realisation that elephants mourn their dead; because of this, whole family groups were taken out whenever possible, except in some cases when calves were spared.

In addition to closing off access points, other measures were taken to reduce the risk of upsetting the public. Large trucks would transport the carcasses, and they all carried tarpaulins to hide the dead animals from view. Special blood-catching tanks were fitted underneath the trucks to avoid leaving trails on roads; adult bulls can weigh 6 to 7 tonnes, and females 3 to 4 tonnes, which makes for a lot of blood.

John and Old Joe didn't speak as they followed the recovery convoy, which slowly moved south down the H3 towards Malelane. Each sat lost in his own thoughts, watching the Park go by. From the road, the view took in so much life, but soon there would be carnage, and not for the first time John wondered whether Africa was big enough for humans and wild animals to co-exist. He would save life today, but he would also once again see it extinguished, as humans and animals went head-to-head over the increasingly contested, limited supply of land and resources.

Old Joe's thoughts were different: he was already thinking of the orphans that the cull would produce. He related to all creatures, human or animal, in almost the same way. He talked to both man and beast silently in his head, and he knew the animals, in particular, heard and understood him. On many occasions John and Jenny Brooker had marvelled at the way animals behaved around Old Joe. But to Old Joe there was nothing to marvel at, he was simply communicating with fellow 'beings'.

The men sat with their thoughts as they headed for the turn-off from the tarmac onto a graded surface, and approached the killing zone.

The helicopter maintained its distance from the herd but kept the elephants in sight so that when the recovery vehicles arrived, it could go into action immediately.

Bully's mother kept her group moving slowly away from the noise in the sky – it was a disturbing irritant from which the whole group wanted to get away. They knew the noise meant potential danger, but after the first time it had not come too close again, so perhaps the danger was not immediate. However, with the noise persisting, their initial puzzlement was turning to fear.

Bully was miserable. He stayed close to his mother as the group moved slowly away from the helicopter noise. He sensed his mother's uncertainty and knew that every elephant in the group felt it too. Bully's world of kindness, affection, playing and fun was soon to be replaced by a new world of panic and darkness.

Bully stayed close to his mother, sensing her uncertainty.

Bully's mother kept her group
moving slowly away
from the noise in the sky.

The machine descended towards the herd, which started to move off in panic.

# 3

# DARKNESS, THE CULL

uxamethonium chloride was a paralysing drug often used to dart elephants from the air. The fully conscious but immobilised animals would go down after a few minutes and then wait helplessly until gun teams came to finish them off. This drug was used in preference to others because the meat of the animal remained fit for human consumption. However, as it was only a paralysing agent, it also meant a two-step operation, which put the elephants through massive stress as they watched the guns finishing off the other animals while they waited for their own bullet.

For this reason, the use of suxamethonium chloride had been abandoned even before culling stopped in the Kruger Park in 1994, and only rifles were used; the simplified operation was marginally more humane.

Although the drug had started to be phased out by the time of Bully's cull, it is likely that darting with muscle relaxant before despatching with rifles was carried out on that fateful day.

Like its Russian counterpart the AK-47, the FN-7.62 millimetre FAL rifle is a weapon of war. It is no accident that two of the most successful military weapons of all time were also to become those most widely used to kill Africa's game animals. The calibre of the Belgian-designed NATO standard FAL is 7.62 x 51 millimetre, while the Russian weapon is 7.62 x 39 millimetre, which means a smaller bullet. The FAL has a rate of fire of 650–700 rounds per minute, a muzzle velocity of 823 metres/second (2,700 feet/second), a bullet weight of 9.30 grams and its magazine takes 20 rounds of ammunition. Although the FAL's bullet is lighter than the very heavy rounds favoured by elephant hunters, when all its specifications are combined it emerges as the ideal tool for culling elephants.

The Bell Jet Ranger is a fast, light helicopter which, on this day, carried a pilot and a marksman. The marksman was the ranger in charge of the section where the cull was to take place. He sat behind the pilot so that he had the same angle of view and effectively would see what the pilot was seeing. As well as providing a platform for the shooter, the helicopter also had to keep circling the animals to keep them bunched up.

The machine descended towards the herd, which started to move off in panic.

Bully's mother looked up as the tone of the helicopter's engine changed and it flew down to her. She couldn't see it yet but her ears and other senses transmitted their message of terrible danger. Bully was at her side when she shook her head, flapped her ears, raised her tail and started to run away from what she knew was a mortal threat.

The whole group got the message and followed Bully's mother in headlong flight. The pilot was experienced and was expecting the elephants to run. He had identified Bully's mother as the matriarch and dived straight at her to turn and then stop her.

Now she saw the machine and half stopped to shake her head, then trumpet her rage and terror. She turned and set off again with the group pounding after her. Little Bully had forgotten games and play; his only concern now was running fast enough to keep up with his mother. The combination of 14 panicked elephants in full flight and the downdraught from the helicopter had produced clouds of choking dust. Bully's light-filled world of happiness was becoming a dark, confusing, frightening nightmare.

The machine's shadow chased Bully's mother on the ground as again she tried to break away from its relentless pursuit. Wherever she turned, the machine and its shadow followed, and only minutes after it first swooped down the helicopter had effectively corralled the group from the air into a terrified screaming and milling throng.

The matriarch is always taken first as this keeps the group together and prevents them from running. There must be no mistakes with the matriarch. Shooting a moving animal from a moving platform required practiced skill. Bully's mother would have to be taken with a clean brain shot so that she would drop on the spot. The placing of the suxamethonium chloride dart did not have to be as precise as a bullet, so was a safer option to guarantee putting her down.

The helicopter circled the group of elephants, keeping them together, and the dart gunner took aim at Bully's mother. The gun fired its .22-calibre blank that powered the dart, and a couple of minutes later, the huge grey animal stopped in mid-stride as her front legs collapsed under her. She went down, then rolled slightly onto her side, paralysed but still fully conscious. Little Bully ran frantically around at his mother's head. He knew she was still alive and reached out his little trunk to touch her head below her eye. She watched, blinked, and it seemed that a tear rolled down as she felt her son's confusion and distress. The pilot and the ranger now worked fast and in concert, as the pilot flew to keep the herd together while the ranger continued darting the elephants with muscle relaxant.

The herd wouldn't leave the matriarch and the adults went down one by one. The recovery team's Land Rovers were now at the cull site and rangers and butchers dismounted to help bring the operation to the speediest possible conclusion.

Minutes earlier there had been 14 live elephants. Now only two adults stood, trumpeting their defiance and terror. Then, seconds later, they too were down and dead with 7.62-millimetre rounds in their brains. Bully, his mother, and the two baby calves were still alive, and for the matriarch the distress was terrible. She heard the confused, frightened cries of the other babies as they tried to understand why their mothers now lay unmoving and dead. The air was filled with the smell of blood and dust, and with the shouts of men and the trumpeting squeals of the baby elephants. A ranger with a 9-millimetre pistol and a rifle walked quickly among the dead and dying elephants, putting final bullets into their heads.

The matriarch watched her frightened little son scamper before her still-seeing eyes, and he was the last thing she saw before a ranger held a rifle to her head and ended her life with a single shot.

John Brooker sat on a rock and stared at the scene of carnage below him as the butchers cut the throats of the dead elephants and removed their intestines. The last animals darted from the air were the calves, which were now down, lying near their dead mothers. Bully and his mother lay a few yards away from the main group of grey bodies and, as someone with long experience of elephants, John

John sat on a rock and stared at the carnage.

was able to appreciate what a truly magnificent specimen she was. She had fallen awkwardly, only partly onto her side because her tusks had dug into the earth when she first went down. The butchers hadn't got to her yet, and he could neither see the dart hanging from her rump, nor the tiny hole in her head where the bullet had entered. She looked perfect, almost as if sleeping, but at an awkward angle.

No matter how tough they are, real men with hearts and souls cry, and tears streamed down John's face, making clear streaks through the dust on his cheeks. He almost wanted to tell the butchers to leave this primal mother alone, not to touch her because it didn't seem right or fair that she should be mutilated. Almost paralysed with grief himself, he just sat there and absorbed the scene, the tragic waste of life, and he feared for the future of elephants in Africa.

An experienced bushman and a pragmatist, he knew and understood all the arguments around culling. As he stared at the dead matriarch, more than ever he wished for open spaces large enough for animals like elephants to live in viable ecosystems that regulated themselves without needing interference from humans. Old Joe came up and stood behind him, and then they walked together to take charge of the orphans.

The road leading to and from the cull site.

Baby elephants, even when only a few weeks old, are very powerful and often teams of strong men struggle to control them. This was why the calves had been darted so they could more easily be put into sling harnesses and lowered into crates. After this they were given antidotes so that they would be on their feet and able to balance during the journey to Skukuza.

Winches and other heavy loading gear were used to get the carcasses into the waiting trucks. The whole herd of 11 dead elephants weighed just under 23 tonnes, and this weight was distributed among the heavy vehicles. By the time tarpaulins were placed over the top of the grisly cargo, the special blood-catching tanks were already starting to fill.

The abattoir at Skukuza would reduce the carcasses to skin, ivory, bone and meat. The ivory would be stored in high-security strong rooms, the bone ground down for meal, the skin had many leather uses, and the meat would be consumed by both humans and animals.

All three calves were strangely silent. As they stood in their crates it was as if the drama and horror of the devastation of their family had struck them dumb. From the time the helicopter pilot picked out Bully's mother as the matriarch, to the time the truck engines started to begin the return journey was just under an hour.

John started his vehicle to drive back to the road and join the convoy. One of the wheels went over a rock and the vehicle lurched, causing John and Old Joe both to turn their heads to make sure the crates were still secure. As they watched, a tiny trunk came out between the bars of one of the crates and seemed to test the surroundings. Dust and the smell of blood and offal were still hanging heavily in the air, and Bully seemed to be trying to understand what had happened – or was he filing away a memory for the rest of his life?

As the vehicle's front wheels left the track and bumped onto the road, the little elephant gave out a high-pitched, squealing trumpet as if he were saying goodbye to his mother and his family group.

The culling of elephants was a brutal business; it was not done for fun or to satisfy bloodlust. Although many fences have since come down, in the late 1980s and early 1990s they were still there, and so was the belief that the main grazing and browsing species – and elephants in particular – had to have their numbers controlled at sustainable levels. It was done with regret, and only because it was genuinely thought to be a necessary management measure that would ultimately be to the benefit of all the Park's wildlife.

The baby calves were now being driven to new and uncertain futures, but they would have futures. It took three hours to cover the 75 kilometres back to Skukuza. All the way, Bully and the others were braced against the movement of the vehicle so that they stayed on their feet. Every now and then a little trunk would appear and wave about as if trying to discover where they were going, or perhaps as a call for help.

On the drive to Skukuza, Old Joe was already having imagined conversations with the calves. A few kilometres before they reached the holding pens, he was telling them that they would soon be unloaded and were to behave themselves. As if in reply a little trunk appeared and there was an ear-splitting trumpeting squeal. Old Joe turned and grinned at John and the heaviness and melancholy between the two men lifted as their thoughts moved swiftly to the mammoth task ahead of keeping the orphans alive and giving them a future.

NASIONALE KRUGERWILDTUIN

## ORPEN

KRUGER NATIONAL PARK

WELCOME TO
ORPEN

TOTAL

The Kruger's Orpen
Gate, where the calves
left their wild lives behind.

# 4

# SKUKUZA AND GLEN AFRIC

lephants have four feet on the ground; humans have only two.
In a pushing-and-shoving contest, elephants will always win.
This was clearly demonstrated upon arrival at Skukuza.

The three crates were offloaded and positioned so that when their sliding gates were opened the baby elephants walked out into the holding pen. The pens were located in a covered area and all three calves were put in the same one. They had not fed for several hours. John knew that if he was to succeed in keeping these animals alive, he had to get them feeding very quickly – not only for sustenance, but also because it would help alleviate stress and trauma.

A bovine (cow's) milk substitute was used in a 2-litre bottle with a large teat. Once the calves realised what these bottles contained, they attacked them hungrily. This was not a refined exercise: John, Old Joe and a helper had a bottle each and soon learnt that the baby elephants made a professional rugby scrum look like child's play.

The South African Springbok rugby team scrum weighs a total of roughly 900 kilograms. The combined weight of the three humans and the three calves was not much lighter, at approximately 750 kilograms. However, considerably more than half this weight was on the side of the elephants, which also had the advantage of having 12 of the 18 feet on the ground. For John, Old Joe and their helper, just staying on their feet was a major achievement.

The calves didn't realise that all three bottles were the same and often decided they wanted to try one of the others' bottles. This meant swapping to a bottle already in use by another calf, involving pushing and shoving that calf out of the way. They didn't all finish their bottles at the same time, and as soon as a calf had finished its bottle, it went looking for another. This meant more pushing and shoving, and more bruises for the humans. Although he was the youngest and the smallest, Bully was not going to miss out and gave as good as he got in feeding sessions.

The calves needed names and the two females each had numbers painted on their ears – one had the number 'Five' and the other 'Three'. They became known as Five and Three, and the names stuck for the rest of their lives. The third was the bull calf and, as with the others, why use imagination when an obvious solution presented itself? The little bull became 'Bully'!

After the first two feeding sessions John started to realise he would have to change things if both calves and humans were to survive intact. The humans were not only collecting sensational bruises, they were also at real risk of broken bones. The little elephants became almost aggressive at feeding times; in addition to pushing and shoving, they started to fight with each other. Elephants weigh 80–100 kilograms at birth, and Five, who was the largest calf, now weighed nearly 200 kilograms – over double the weight of the average human. At this stage Bully was still the smallest, but at approximately 150 kilograms he weighed much more than either John or Old Joe.

They tried to feed the calves at three- to four-hourly intervals through the night, and by morning both John and Old Joe were 'dead on their feet'. During one of the intervals between feeding John lay on his bed trying to work out the answers that would give the calves a chance. He realised they would have to be penned separately, so they could be fed in safety, and he could make sure that each calf was getting enough milk. An alarming new development was that all three calves had developed diarrhoea, and while John knew that stress was the most likely cause, he also knew that bovine milk substitute would not be a long-term solution, and could already be causing problems. Diarrhoea would lead to dehydration, which eventually would lead to death. He would need to monitor their droppings individually and this was another reason why separate pens were needed as soon as possible. He made his decision; he had to get the calves back to his base at Glen Afric near Johannesburg as soon as possible.

Between feeding sessions John and Old Joe made preparations to move the elephants the next day. John asked for help from SANParks in arranging permits to transport the calves, and alerted the staff at Glen Afric to the imminent arrival of Bully, Five and Three. Years of moving game animals had taught John many lessons and he had incorporated this experience in the design of his own special high-speed game truck. Powered by CAT and built by Oshkosh, the truck had 13 forward gears and could cruise at speeds of up to 120 kilometres an hour. Each calf would have a separate compartment for the journey to their new home at Glen Afric.

Twenty-four hours after the cull and their arrival at Skukuza, all three calves still had diarrhoea, and it was getting worse. At this stage John wasn't sure whether the major cause was stress or the bovine milk substitute. He knew that the stress would pass as the calves settled, but he had to keep them alive while he looked for answers, so the feeding continued even though he suspected the milk powder itself might be poisoning them. It was a vicious circle: the trauma of the cull had caused massive stress, and now the diarrhoea was causing further stress, weight loss, and dehydration.

As dawn broke on the second day after the cull, John and Old Joe prepared to load the calves and begin a race against time to save their lives. The staff at Glen Afric had been told to buy every different type of milk powder they could, both human and animal. As soon as he got back to Glen Afric, John wanted to study the contents of the milk powders, talk to his vets and other experts, and start looking for a solution. The calves were slightly sedated to make it easier to load them for the journey. The compartment floors were padded with straw, and the calves given a final pre-journey feed.

Soon John, Old Joe, Bully, Five and Three were on board the Oshkosh and heading for the Orpen Gate where they would leave the Park. This was the second time in their short lives the calves had to balance against the motion of a moving platform, and it wasn't long before they not only got used to it but found the motion and the engine noise comforting.

They didn't know it but, as they went through the Orpen Gate, they were leaving their wild lives behind. Beyond the Park boundary the calves started new lives in which the first challenge would be to survive, and the second would be growing up in a human, rather than an elephant, world.

Glen Afric was a wild animal holding area and a United States Department of Agriculture (USDA)-approved quarantine centre. From here, wild animals were exported to zoos and parks all over the world, and animals being imported to South Africa were held in quarantine. When a safari park was opened in Thailand, the entire complement of animals was processed through Glen Afric prior to being exported. On another occasion, over 200 Bovine TB-free buffalo were brought from all over the world and quarantined at Glen Afric before being sent on to various southern African destinations. The facilities were extensive and the staff highly trained and very experienced. If John were to beat the odds and keep Bully, Five and Three alive, he knew he would need all of Glen Afric's facilities and staff resources.

They would travel the 500 kilometres without stopping. The truck was fast but along many sections the road wasn't good, so the journey would take at least six hours. First they drove west and then turned south, passing through Sabie and then over the Long Tom Pass on their way to join the N4, turning west again for Pretoria and Johannesburg. Glen Afric is located outside Johannesburg near Broederstroom, near the Hartbeespoort Dam, and is just off the R512.

They had a good run and pulled into the Glen Afric farm just before 1.00 p.m. John's family and the staff were waiting and quickly moved into action. The little elephants were unloaded and in their individual holding pens within minutes. The compartments on the truck were foul, but before they were cleared out John wanted to look at the straw. There was a considerable amount of fluid in each compartment, and the urine and liquid faeces indicated that dehydration was not something to worry about just in the future: it was a real problem already. The one piece of good news was the lack of blood; had this been present it would have indicated the start of structural damage to the calves' digestive systems, which would have added another dimension to the existing veterinary problems.

The next few days were a sleepless nightmare for John and his teams of helpers. Old Joe, however, was a miracle: he didn't seem to need sleep and stayed up through the nights talking to his calves. The baby elephants knew they were in trouble. They were getting steadily weaker as the days went by and John grappled with finding an acceptable milk solution. Diarrhoea and the ensuing weakness was clearly causing the calves distress and John knew he could lose them soon.

Despite their weakness and discomfort, they responded to Old Joe. He was always talking to them, whether audibly or in his head. He told them not to give up because everything would come out right and they would get better. They would greet his approach with noises and sometimes by raising their little trunks. Old Joe had become their mother, father, best friend and herd bull, and in some weird way he knew, he absolutely knew for certain they would pull through – he trusted John completely and just accepted he would find an answer. Somehow, Old Joe passed this confidence in John on to the calves and, although they got weaker, they fought to stay alive.

John had tried all the milk powders he could find. He had consulted his vets and researched work done by Daphne Sheldrick and others. He had noted the contents of all the milk powders and monitored the calves' reaction to each one.

Since their arrival at the farm, the calves had been in separate pens. This completely alleviated the pushing, shoving and fighting problems, and also meant that each calf's urine and dung could be analysed separately.

As the days passed, a combination of trial and error, careful record keeping and guesswork led John to the conclusion that, while elephant milk is very high in butter fat, the calves' stomachs could not absorb butter fat from other species, the prime culprit being bovine butter fat. They would drink greedily but diarrhoea always followed immediately. The reaction to some milk powders was better than others, and eventually John settled on a human weight-watchers milk substitute called Weigh-Less.

This product contained only 0.2 percent butter fat and, although diarrhoea persisted, it was not as bad as on other products, which gave John a foundation on which to build. Brown rice was liquidised and added to the milk powder to provide bulk and carbohydrate. This produced a new problem: the mixture was now too thick to pass through the teats on the 2-litre bottles. John and Old Joe decided to put the mixture into buckets, and the calves learnt to suck through soft, clear hose pipes.

John would never have described himself as a particularly emotional man; neither did he think of himself as a raving lunatic. However, both possibilities went through his mind when, late one afternoon, he awoke from a catnap, opened his fridge door and simultaneously burst out laughing and crying at the sight of a plateful of elephant dung. Solid elephant dung! He had won, he would save his calves. He wasn't sure who had sent him this unusual but welcome message, but the prime suspect had to be Old Joe.

He went to the elephant pens and Old Joe was there, talking to his calves while cleaning out Five's pen. The smell was different, the whole atmosphere was different, and the floors in the pens were dry. Bully's little trunk came snaking through the bars and John stopped to have a look at him. The little bull was brighter, stronger looking, and seemed to know he had won perhaps the most important battle of his life. Probiotics, electrolytes, anti-diarrhoeal medicine, vitamin E, selenium and other supplements were added, and within a few days it was as if there had never been a life-threatening crisis.

Since their arrival the baby elephants had been at the centre of life at Glen Afric, and now that their diet had been resolved, everyone on the farm went about their work with a spring in their step. John's formula had saved the calves, and as they got stronger and more demanding, food preparation and the four-hourly feeding of three hungry elephants became a full-time job for Old Joe and a helper. The feeding equipment and pens were kept scrupulously clean, and Old Joe personally supervised every aspect of the elephants' care.

The three calves were all that was left of the family group. They were penned beside each other, could see each other, and showed signs of needing to be together. The feeding battle had been won, and John could turn his mind to helping the mental scars to heal. The only benefit of their sickness was that they had fast come to trust their new human family, and Bully, in particular, had developed a bond with Old Joe.

Eleven days after arriving at Glen Afric, Bully, Five and Three were ready to take the next step in their new lives.

# 5
# GROWING UP - A NEW FAMILY

**H**umans and elephants are two of Earth's longest-living mammals, and in their development and growing up stages the two species have much in common.

Despite their longevity and intelligence, humans get off to a very slow start. Human babies remain recumbent, immobile, and totally dependent on adults for many months. In contrast, elephants are on their feet and independently mobile within hours of being born, and are playing with their peers within weeks. However, once humans have caught up, the stages of infancy, childhood, teenage years and adolescence are very similar to the corresponding stages in elephant development.

Bully, Three and Five would now have to grow up without the benefit of help and instruction from elders of their own species. No matter how good a job John, Old Joe and others did, they would never be able to replicate the education that young elephants gain growing up in their family groups.

Elephants communicate using a range of sounds that effectively form a language with a varied vocabulary. Language is thought to be taught to youngsters by the matriarch and the senior female members of the herd.

The herd bull teaches discipline and acceptable behaviour to the young males. Shows of bad behaviour – such as adolescent bulls inexplicably attacking, and sometimes killing, other species and even other elephants – have often pointed to the absence of a dominant adult male; and only when a mature bull is introduced to the area does the situation calm down, and unruly male teenagers learn how to behave properly. Older youngsters remember how they were disciplined when play became too boisterous or annoying, and pass these lessons on to the younger animals.

Human teachers would now do their best to educate Bully, Three and Five, but it was inevitable that the calves would grow up lacking a great deal of elephant knowledge. Humans certainly can successfully raise wild animals, but there is no doubt that they create very different creatures from the truly wild members of the species. This is an important aspect in the debate over whether humans should intervene and rear wild animals in captivity or semi-captivity. In the case of animals as intelligent as elephants, there's a strong argument that depriving them of their natural wild life, and their normal elephant education, can be so damaging that in many cases it would have been better had they died with their family group.

A lot more is known now about elephant behaviour, intelligence, communication and social structures than was known in the early 1990s. Had John Brooker and others known then what is known now, it's debatable whether they would have agreed to save the calves for a life in captivity.

Eleven days after the cull, three strong and healthy baby elephants were desperate to escape the confines of their pens and play together. They had become accustomed to their four-hourly milk and rice feeds and their body clocks knew precisely when the next feed was due.

Although humans can't control baby elephant calves with strength, John was confident they could be controlled in other ways, and feeding times was one of them. Bully, Three and Five had all formed close bonds with Old Joe and the other grooms.

The baby elephants were initially confined to pens.

Bully and friends growing up at Glen Afric.

Old Joe, in particular, had an almost mystical relationship with all three calves, but especially with Bully. Day 12 was the day of release from the pens and a small crowd of onlookers had gathered to see what would happen when the gates were opened. The excitement and expectancy in the air was almost palpable as three grooms simultaneously opened all three pens. People held their breath as the gates opened all the way and then ... nothing happened! There was no mad dash for freedom: instead, three little elephants stood looking uncertain, and John burst out laughing.

Bully, Five and Three had lost their mothers and their family group, they were captive, in a strange place, and had almost died. The pens had become their safe havens, and trumpeting to get out was one thing, but actually taking those giant steps was another. The frozen tableau lasted only seconds before John and Old Joe walked towards the pens and called the calves out.

Five was the first out, then Bully exploded from his pen and chased after her, and was immediately followed by Three. They touched with their trunks and nuzzled each other; then, confused, but starting to thaw, they gave John and Old Joe the same gentle recognition and greeting treatment. During the next four hours John and Old Joe stayed with the calves as they gradually became bolder and started to play and explore their new surroundings.

In the wild the babies had been kept moving all day as the herd browsed, grazed, mud- and sand-bathed, played in water, drank and went about elephant business. For the last 12 days this natural routine had been missing and John was relieved and happy that it had now been restored. After three and a half hours of play and exploration the calves seemed to know it was feed time, and they obediently followed John and Old Joe back to the holding area.

In bed that night, after the calves' first day out, John had his first worry-free, full night's sleep since the cull. The calves were feeding well and obviously would adapt to a daily release programme. The first steps had been taken towards giving the orphans a future.

As a character, Bully stood out. He was the naughtiest, fastest and greediest of the three calves. It was quite impossible not to be captivated by him, as a late-night feeding story illustrates. After the late feed, Five and Three would lie down and go to sleep. Bully refused, and used to cry out if left alone. Whoever had given the feed would have to come and stroke him. One night John was fussing over him and he caught John's fingers and sucked them. This calmed him down and he slowly fell asleep as he sucked. This became an established nightly routine: whoever gave the late-evening feed would have to stay with Bully and let him suck their fingers as he slowly slid to the floor.

This meant that the owner of the fingers had to bend down so that they stayed in Bully's mouth as he gradually sank down and fell asleep on the floor – otherwise he would wake up again. This bed-time ritual went on for a couple of months and to this day, John regrets not having filmed or photographed this elephant version of sucking a dummy!

Every morning after the seven o'clock feed a weird and surreal scene was enacted as Old Joe led his elephants out to play like an old Pied Piper. The calves were growing fast, and even Bully, who was still the smallest, weighted four or five times more than Old Joe. Elephant calf play can be fast and boisterous, and Old Joe was often nearly caught in the crossfire of calf chasing and wrestling contests, but never once did they pose any threat to him. If Bully or any of the others was being silly or misbehaving, a rebuke from Old Joe was all that was needed to correct the situation. Bully was most often the culprit and a simple 'Come on Bully, you are being stupid now' usually did the trick.

Glen Afric is 750 hectares and, as the weeks became months, the elephants expanded their daily range until they roamed the whole farm area. The dam was their favourite place and John never tired

The dam was their favourite place
and John never tired of watching
them play in the water.

of watching them play in the water. Dust- and mud-baths were also very popular, and if Old Joe couldn't hear or see them, he could still easily find them by following their trail, or by visiting their favourite play sites.

Memories of the cull and the loss of their family receded but didn't disappear as they slowly adjusted to their lives with humans. Old Joe would let them out in the morning and they would wander off and come back when they felt like it. Bully, Five and Three didn't realise it, but they had been unwitting pioneers, and were about to become trail blazers.

By the beginning of summer, at four to five months old, the calves were settled in their routine. Five was clearly the leader as she was the oldest and cleverest; however, Bully had overtaken the others in size and was now the largest. What the calves didn't know was that BMW had sponsored John to take more orphans from Kruger Park culls. Before BMW had made the offer John had decided he wouldn't rear any more calves. Saving them was one thing, but he worried where they would end up because he couldn't keep them all. On the other hand, he realised the BMW offer would allow him to perfect his rearing techniques. This changed his mind because he saw a value for all calves, whether the victims of culls, or zoo animals that had lost their mothers, or those orphaned by mortality in the wild.

During the rest of 1992, 11 more Kruger orphans were brought back to Glen Afric. Bully, Five and Three now had a new dimension to their lives: they were teachers and role models. The new calves all took to the milk formula without much trouble, and they learnt how to drink it from the buckets through the hoses by watching the older calves.

The new babies arrived in ones, twos and threes until the end of the year, and John is very proud that he didn't lose a single calf. They all thrived and Old Joe became the most important figure in their lives.

At around nine or 10 months John and Old Joe noticed that Bully, Five and Three had started to browse and graze. They would take leaves off trees and occasionally pull up grass. They were starting the process of weaning themselves off milk, and were sending a message to their human handlers.

They continued getting their rice/milk feeds, but slowly lucerne and hay were introduced to their diet. Keeping and rearing 14 baby elephants should have been a massive undertaking, almost a Mission Impossible. The volume of food being consumed was huge, and the daily husbandry requirements demanding, but the work was made much lighter thanks to Bully, Five and Three. They showed the babies how to feed, they gave them comfort and confidence, and showed them the daily routines.

Old Joe's Pied Piper performance had become an even more extraordinary sight by the end of the year as 14 little elephants followed their human leader out into the bush each day.

It was a remarkable achievement for both humans and elephants that, despite all the potential hazards, the management challenges and the large number of elephants, there were no serious accidents or life-threatening incidents.

Old Joe was the key figure in the calves' lives, but they were lucky that at Glen Afric there were many other experienced animal handlers too: Phineas, Little Joe and Lucas were also close to the young elephants, and helped in bringing them up.

All wild animals are different and each species has its own problems and needs. Due to their intelligence and size, elephants are perhaps the most complex and demanding if they are to have a good quality of life and remain manageable. This meant the grooms had to take into account many factors when handling their young charges.

Identifying males and females was initially difficult because bull

Bully with his handler Lucas.

elephants have no scrotum, which meant that identifying males from females at a glance was not possible. The trunk, which is a fusion of the upper lip and the nose, can be used to give handlers a healthy whack, or to spray them with water and dust. Trunks can also be used to throw objects, and Bully, in particular, developed a deadly accurate aim with whatever he chose to throw.

Trumpeting is achieved by forcing air through the trunk so violently that the nasal mucosa and septum resonate. The sound is amplified as it passes down the long tunnels of the trunk. Trumpeting usually expresses fear or anger, but can happen during play, social interactions, and to express excitement. At one time or another all of the calves' handlers found out just how ear-splitting trumpeting can be if you are standing too close!

Elephants saved by John and Jenny Brooker from the Kruger Park culls have ended up all over the world. The Brookers still remember many of their names: Bully, Five, Three, Mopani, Letaba, Jack, Rogan, Rambo, Tooth and Rachel. They don't know where all the elephants are now: Bully is still in South Africa, and they think Mopani is too – in the Elephant Sanctuary; Jack and Tooth are in Germany, and Five and Letaba are in the West Midlands Safari Park in the UK.

On 5 May, 2014, Five gave birth to a 100-kilogram bull calf. The calf was the first baby elephant born at the Park in its 41-year history, and has proved to be a big attraction and a great favourite with the public. Five was impregnated using frozen semen from a South African bull, and her calf is only the second to be born in captivity anywhere in the world using this technique; the first was born at Vienna Zoo in 2013.

Other surviving calves from the Kruger culls of the early 1990s can be found in parks and reserves all over South Africa, including Inverdoorn, Fairy Glen, Aquila, The Knysna Elephant Park, The Elephant Sanctuary and others.

Was it justified to rescue these elephants as calves?

The key question is, how well adjusted are the ones living in captivity? We will never know to what degree they miss their wild lives. However, with animals as intelligent as elephants, possessing long memories, and ways of talking to each other, there must be a great chance that they realise they are, in fact, prisoners in captivity.

Human prisoners do their time, but most can look forward to being released one day; sadly, the same is not true for the majority of captive elephants. They are serving life sentences and may just be aware of their fate. Was it justified to rescue them as calves?

John Brooker acknowledges the debate and its validity. He points out that our knowledge of elephants and understanding of their intelligence is much greater now than it was 24 years ago, in 1991. By agreeing to save the orphans, he believes he took a life-over-death decision based on the knowledge of the day; were he faced with the same situation today, he would assess it with the benefit of our current knowledge and understanding. Brooker believes that, in general, life is preferable to death; but this holds only if the elephants are kept in appropriate conditions, and treated with kindness, sensitivity and consideration.

From the TV series 'Wild at Heart'

# 6

# FILMS AND TV COMMERCIALS

As a skilled and experienced animal handler and capturer, it was perhaps inevitable that John would become involved in filming and photo shoots with his animals.

Bully appeared in nearly 30 films, TV ads and photo shoots between 1992 and his 'film star' retirement in 2008, when he was 16. His charm, cheek and naughtiness made him a natural in front of the camera. Other handlers could work with Bully, but John, Old Joe and, later, Lucas were trusted by him, and one of them was always present when he was being filmed.

The use of trained but once-wild animals to entertain humans has been a hot topic of debate for many years. Animals performing in circuses has now been banned in many countries, and the conditions under which animals are filmed is usually strictly controlled. Sadly, there are still places where animals perform for humans and are trained to do so using methods that can involve great cruelty. John and Jenny Brooker adhere to the highest standards, and the welfare of their animals always takes precedence over other considerations.

Most of Bully's appearances are listed in the following pages. Among these were some particularly notable or amusing performances, which are described in greater detail later in this chapter.

## 1992/ – 'OKAVANGO'

Bully and other young orphan elephants at Glen Afric were often seen in this US TV series, starring Steve Kanaley, Connie Nielsen and Michelle Scarabelli.

## 1993/4 – ISM ADVERTISEMENT – ELEPHANTS HATCHING

During the period of restricted trading with South Africa due to apartheid, the computer giant IBM pulled out of the country and ISM took its place. This TV commercial for ISM featured Bully and a few baby elephant 'colleagues' hatching out of giant eggshells in the desert. This symbolised new ideas and a new start. (At the time of writing, the ad could still be viewed on YouTube, and it does look faintly ridiculous, but Bully hatched with great skill!)

## 1995 – 'SOLDIER, SOLDIER'

During the filming of 'Soldier Soldier' for British TV, a group of 'soldiers' were lying camouflaged in the grass in an observation/ambush position. They couldn't be picked up by the camera, and there were wildebeest, zebra, and giraffe grazing in the background. Then the actors were required to stand up from where they had been hiding and to walk slowly off out of shot.

The director shot the scene twice and was quite happy with it, but John suggested one more go to improve it by using the elephants as well as the other animals.

Old Joe fetched the elephants, and the actors again lay down in their positions. The carer held the elephants in readiness to move across the camera and, when 'ACTION' was announced, John called the group of five or six elephants, at the back of which was Bully.

All started out according to plan and, as the elephants came into the shot, the actors rose up out of the grass. This surprised the elephants, which took off in panic, exactly as planned – except for Bully. He turned, stared at the actors, flapped his ears, and let forth an ear-splitting trumpeting. Terrified actors ran in one direction and Bully went in the other. Unplanned, unscripted and unrehearsed, this was spontaneous and convincing footage. Bully had helped to nail a very impressive scene. John and the director were delighted, but the actors could probably have done without the real-life close encounter!

## 1997 – 'JOCK OF THE BUSHVELD'

The story of Jock, the Staffordshire bull terrier, is a famous and well-loved tale in South Africa. The book was made into a film in 1997, starring the late Jonathan Rands, and Bully put in a brief appearance.

## 1998 – SUN CITY PALACE

Bully was one of the backdrop animals in this TV commercial.

## 1998 – PLASCON WALL & ALL – TV ADVERTISEMENT

Dream parts for Bully, Three and Mopani: all they had to do in this ad for the paint manufacturer Plascon was to throw mud at a wall. They did it very well and with great enthusiasm – a natural role for elephants!

## 1998 – GARDEN COURT HOLIDAY INN – LAUNCH DINNER FOR TFC TOURS

In this live performance at a black tie dinner held at the Garden Court Holiday Inn to launch TFC tours, Bully and John walked through a 'solid wall' to make a dramatic entrance on stage in front of a packed dining room full of invited guests. The wall was actually made of polystyrene, and John told me that it was huge fun and he wasn't sure who enjoyed it more, him or Bully.

## 1999 – STILLS SHOOT FOR *MAXIM* MAGAZINES (ANGELINA JOLIE)

Angelina Jolie is one of the world's biggest stars. In April 2000, *Maxim* magazine launched in South Africa with a special edition, and Angelina Jolie and Bully were hired for the photo shoot. If Bully was impressed by appearing alongside such glamour and talent, he didn't show it. As usual, John and Old Joe directed his performance; and, as usual, Bully went through his paces like a professional.

## 1999 – MISS TEEN PAGEANT

In 1999 the final of Miss Teen, South Africa, was held at Vodaworld, and at the end, after the young beauty queen had been chosen, John, Jenny, Bully, Three and two young lions all joined the winner on stage to congratulate her and celebrate her success.

## 2000 – NOKIA 6250 – TV COMMERCIAL

In 2000 Bully starred in a commercial for Nokia cell phones. The particular model was waterproof and the film had to promote this feature.

A shower was built in the bush so that an actor could be filmed receiving a call and answering it in the shower on his waterproof Nokia cell phone. The caller was actually several hundred yards away in the Lodge, and could be heard saying 'Look behind you'. The actor in the shower turns to find Bully standing behind him. He drops his phone in shock, and it lands in the water on the floor of the shower.

The script then called for Bully to make a 'trunk call'. This involved his picking the phone up with his trunk. John tempted Bully to do this by squeezing an orange over the phone. Bully enthusiastically picked up the orange-smelling and -tasting waterproof Nokia and put it in his mouth. From several yards away John heard an ominous crunch and intervened with 'No Bully, drop it'.

Bully obviously hadn't read the script, or maybe he was working to another script, because dropping it or waving it around in his trunk making a trunk call wasn't what he had in mind. Using his trunk, he retrieved the phone from his mouth, and with an accuracy that would make a professional cricketer envious, he threw it at John. Bully's unscripted throw was bang on target and professional cricketers would also have been proud of John, who caught it apparently effortlessly. 'Cut', said the director, and John walked his cricketing buddy back to his quarters, and gave him a few oranges on the way.

## 2000 – TV SERIES, ST GEORGES ISLAND

This U.S series featured a family from overseas arriving in South Africa to make it their home. The father was a veterinarian and this provided the idea that was later copied in many other series. Bully made various background appearances.

## 2001 – MEDSCHEME – TV MEDICAL INSURANCE COMMERCIAL

This medical insurance commercial was based on a true story when an elephant fell into a hole and got trapped. A ramp was built to rescue the animal and allow it to walk out. The story was re-enacted for the commercial with Bully in the starring role.

## 2001 – 'MR BONES'

The Leon Schuster movie 'Mr Bones', released in 2001, remains one of the most commercially successful South African movies ever produced. Schuster, one of South Africa's leading stars, wrote it, starred in it, and was involved in the screenplay and other aspects of its making.

Bully appears in three scenes. In the first he is constipated and, watched by a shocked tourist group on safari, Schuster plunges his arm into Bully's backside and removes the blockage. Seconds later, Bully evacuates the remaining contents of his bowels with deadly accuracy and covers the tour guide,

and the man who is eventually confirmed to be the heir to the throne of the imaginary kingdom of Kuvukiland. In his second appearance Bully is seen in the bush, and in his third he helps defeat the forces of evil by causing a helicopter full of bad guys to crash. Bully's intervention is the start of things going well, and everything ending in 'happy-ever-after' mode.

## 2001 – JEEP TV COMMERCIAL

Bully and other elephants were filmed in the bush, foraging while a Jeep drove past on a track.

## 2002 – NATIONAL GEOGRAPHIC / DISCOVERY CHANNEL

Animals at Glen Afric were often involved in National Geographic and Discovery shoots, and Bully made regular appearances. By this time the Brookers had evolved a strict policy for the use of their animals in film and TV shoots. The animals would not be made to do tricks, and all filming had to be done on the farm with animals behaving as naturally as possible.

## 2002 – CARTE BLANCHE – TV SHOW

At 10 years old, Bully was showing all the signs that he would develop into a very big bull. Like any growing youngster he could be mischievous, but generally he was a calm, caring, intelligent and sensitive animal. This was demonstrated in front of the camera in his relationship with a young blind girl called Ranschia.

In 2002/03 the TV show Carte Blanche covered attempts by a therapist to use elephants to help children with severe mental and physical disabilities. Ranschia lacked any interest in life and could not be motivated to perform even the simplest of tasks like making her own bed. Bully transformed her. He would let her feel his face and trunk, and in turn would very gently put his trunk all over her. The effect was miraculous and Ranschia became truly alive on her visits to Bully. He became her reward system. If she was good and made her bed and did other chores and her schoolwork, she would be allowed to visit her friend Bully. Of all Bully's performances, his work with Ranschia must rank as his finest. Was it just a performance, or was he showing what a truly remarkable animal he is?

## 2004/12 – 'WILD AT HEART' – UK ITV SERIES

Bully participated in another series, based on St George's Island – the hugely successful ITV show 'Wild at Heart', which starred Hayley Mills, Deon Stewardson, Stephen Tompkinson, Amanda Holden and others.

Bully featured in the early episodes. He was often on camera, wandering around the set built specially for the filming. The show ran for several seasons on ITV before the rights were sold to SKY TV, which is believed to be considering a new series provided the key actors can be re-assembled. The story is about an English vet who brings his family to South Africa and eventually gets involved in trying to run a private game reserve (Leopard's Den) alongside his veterinary practice. His right-hand man is a highly likeable South African rogue called Anders du Plessis.

The human cast worked alongside John Brooker's animals and the cheetahs, lions, elephants, wildebeest, zebra and other residents of Glen Afric were all regularly on camera. One of Bully's most dramatic scenes was when he had to be 'knocked down'. He would need to be fully tranquillised with a drug called M99, fired from the same type of dart gun that had been used when his family was culled.

South African government rules do not allow animals to be darted and tranquillised for filming purposes unless there is a valid veterinary reason. In Bully's case the reason was that Jenny Brooker wanted vets to check on one of his tusks. His left tusk had broken below the skin and had split (see next chapter

– A giant toothache). Veterinary surgeons had removed most of it, but Jenny wanted to be sure there was no infection or abscess, so took the opportunity of Bully's sedation to allow the vets to investigate.

Everything went according to plan and Bully collapsed dramatically and went to sleep. Thankfully he was lying on the opposite side to that of the broken tusk, allowing it to be inspected. If he had gone down the other way, turning such a heavy animal would have been a challenge, even for a film crew.

Filming took longer than expected and the main vet, Dr Gerhard Steenkamp, ran out of time and had to leave. The assessment was eventually carried out by an experienced colleague.

## 2007 – AMSTEL BIG FIVE – TV COMMERCIAL

This TV commercial re-enacted the Noah's Ark story with animals going into an ark two by two.

## 2007 – TRAUM (DREAM HOTEL)

A German TV production, Bully had a minor background part.

## 2007 – 'LIFE IS WILD', US TV SERIES

Once again, St Georges Island was the inspiration. Bully had background parts.

## 2008 – COMMERCIALS FOR SAMSUNG, CITROEN, PPC, OUTSURANCE

This was a busy year for Bully in TV commercials. Notable among these four commissions was the PPC commercial which used the power of an elephant to illustrate the strength of PPC cement. This was Bully's last year of making appearances in front of the camera. John is convinced that he often enjoyed being the centre of attention, and was always very quick to grasp what was required of him.

Bully managed to get involved in most aspects of life in the Brooker family. Together with others he appeared in a commercial filmed in the dark around a camp fire, which involved a well-known actor talking to a young boy about Africa of yesteryear. The scene called for elephants to walk past in the shadows in the background. John was standing behind the camera watching the scene being shot, and Jenny was standing a short distance away. They had only just starting going out and John had high hopes for the relationship.

The scene was shot successfully and in the dark John walked to join Jenny. He hadn't realised Bully was following right behind him, padding along on his huge, silent feet. John came into the light where Jenny was standing, and she asked him how the shoot had gone. Before he could answer, a large trunk snaked over his shoulder and grabbed Jenny.

Her scream was impressive, and John was able to enhance his courtship credentials by rescuing her from the enthusiastic embrace of Bully's trunk.

Bully can be seen in the photograph opposite with a very short left-hand tusk, which reduced his appeal for films, commercials and photo shoots. The Brookers did try to fit an extension but this didn't really work, and he retired from working in front of the camera in 2008.

His tusk problems had started when he was chained up as a younger animal and used his tusk to play with his chain. It was common practice to restrain elephants by fitting a padded collar around an ankle, which was fixed to a chain secured to the floor. The Brookers abandoned this practice many years ago but they were still doing it when Bully was a young elephant.

Jonathan shares a story with Bully.

John and Old Joe were Bully's leaders, but his best human friend was John's young son, Jonathan. From the time he was in a nappy and took his first steps, Jonathan had played with Bully, who would hug him with his trunk, pick him up, and let him run around underneath him and through his legs. Their relationship was one of those extraordinary cross-species friendships, which has to be seen to be believed. The giant elephant and the human baby grew up together and needed each other's company.

When Bully was 10 years old, he broke his chain and so escaped his 'mooring'. The Brooker family suspected at the time that he was looking for Jonathan. After this incident it was noticed he had a loose tusk, and a few months later the vets had to intervene to relieve a giant toothache.

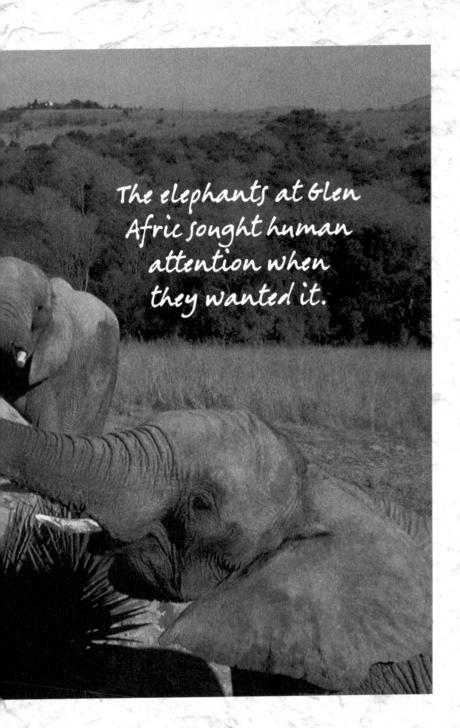

The elephants at Glen Afric sought human attention when they wanted it.

# 7

# A GIANT TOOTHACHE

By the time he was 10 years old, Bully was notching up an impressive CV of 'firsts'. He was in the first batch of calves to be successfully milk-reared by John, was the first elephant known to use a human hand as a sleep-inducing dummy, is one of only a few animals to have worked with both regional and global superstars, and may be the first elephant to have been engaged in therapy for handicapped children, including the blind girl Ranschia.

Another first would be due to his having broken his tusk, and undergoing the first dental operation of its kind in South Africa.

Grooves and scratches in the outer enamel of his tusk showed that Bully regularly played with his chain. Just as humans use either a left or right hand more than the other, so elephants use one tusk as their main one. This is known as the slave tusk and was the tusk Bully had broken. Most of the time he just enjoyed playing with the annoying contraption round his foreleg, but on one occasion he did use his ever-increasing strength to break the chain when he decided to go and visit his young friend Jonathan Brooker.

It is almost certainly in the course of this escape that he cracked his tusk, but it wasn't immediately noticed. Some days, or maybe even weeks later, Jenny Brooker noticed that the tusk was loose and wobbled slightly.

Between 2000 and 2011 Bully would undergo six veterinary interventions to relieve his giant toothaches. There is no doubt that the breakage occurred as a direct result of his being chained up – the customary method of restraining captive elephants in 1999/2000. The Brookers have long since stopped using chains, but in the course of researching this book it emerged that chaining elephants is still common practice elsewhere.

Many would argue that there is nothing wrong with this method of restraint. After all, horses, donkeys, camels and others are tied up or tethered to keep them in one place. The metal collars around elephants' ankles are usually padded and, provided care is taken, most chained elephants don't come to any harm. The tying and tethering of horses and hobbling of camels is accepted, so why should it be different for elephants?

There are two basic differences between horses or camels and elephants. The first is intelligence: it is accepted that elephants possess far greater intelligence, as we understand it, then either horses or camels. The second is that most working horses and camels are beasts of burden, born in captivity. Many captive elephants, and Bully is one of them, were born wild and free, so being restrained by humans is likely to be much more damaging and difficult for them to accept.

The Brookers knew that Bully was suffering. His eyes spoke of pain and he seemed to be saying 'Help me'. By 1997, homes had been found for most of the calves hand-reared by John from Kruger culls; the Glen Afric farm was simply not big enough for all of them. Bully, Three and Mopani had been kept and were effectively members of the Brooker family. When it became obvious that Bully was suffering,

After the first treatment Bully was left
with one tusk shorter than the other.

John and Jenny sought the best possible medical attention, just as
they would have done for one of their children.

On 5 October, 2000, Dr Gerhard Steenkamp, a veterinarian who
has a particular interest in dentistry, carried out the first procedure to
cure Bully's giant toothache.

Elephants have a total of 28 teeth over the course of their life,
including two sets of tusks that are found in the upper jaw only and
are modified incisors. The first of these are milk tusks, which are also
called tushes, and are usually lost and replaced before they become
visible. It was Bully's left tusk, one of his permanent giant incisors,
that Dr Steenkamp had to repair.

Bully was anaesthetised so that a thorough examination and
treatment could be carried out. It was found that the tusk had fractured,
which had led to an abscess forming. The plan was to drill out the oval
centre core, and seal the tooth with a nylon plug that could be removed
by handlers when treatment of the abscess was needed.

Bully was anaesthetised so that a thorough examination and treatment could be carried out.

Dr Steenkamp would see Bully on a further three occasions at Glen Afric. Seven or eight months after the initial operation John and Jenny Brooker again suspected that all was not well: John and Old Joe agreed that, although the tusk seemed to be growing, it was loose

Dr Gerhard Steenkamp

again. Dr Steenkamp was recalled on 19 September, 2001 and, after anaesthetising Bully, discovered that he had cracked his tusk again. Although the Glen Afric elephants were only rarely chained by this time, this convenient method of restraint was still occasionally used and the likelihood is that Bully's second fracture had also been caused by his playing with the chain.

Dr Steenkamp investigates Bully's tusk.

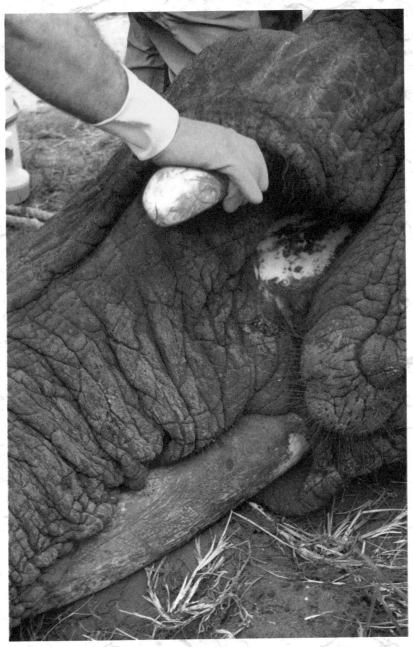

Bully had cracked his tusk again.

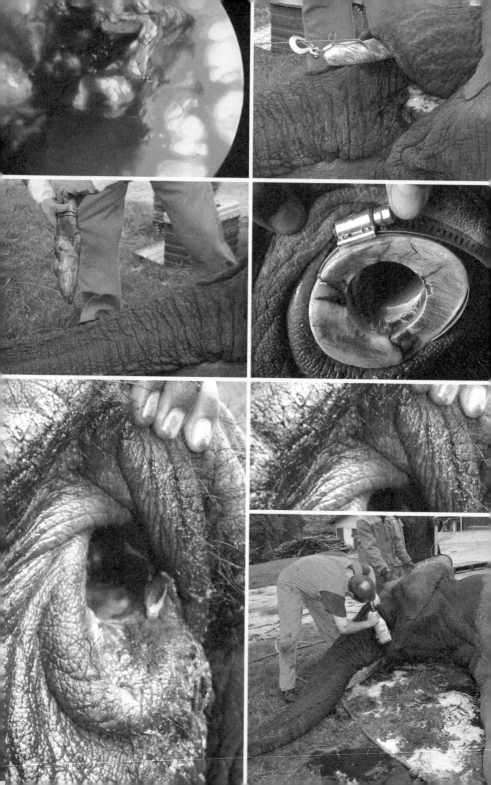

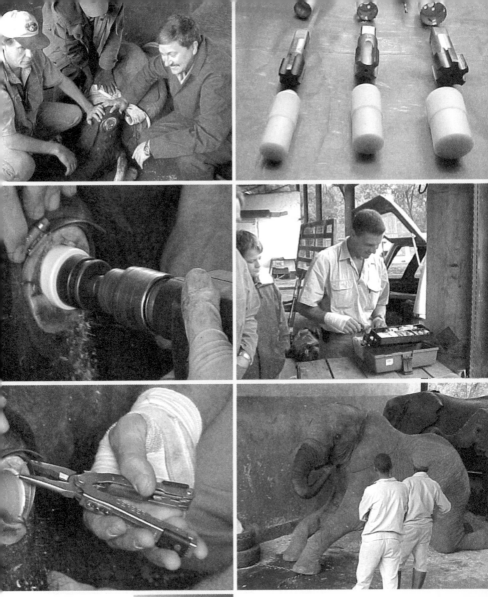

Bully experienced giant toothaches on and off for several years, during which time he added to his list of firsts by becoming a dental-technology guinea pig.

Bully being prepared for his first operation.

Dr Steenkamp pioneered the use of threaded nylon fillings.

Bully was about to add another 'first' to his growing list. Steenkamp had been developing threaded nylon fillings and Bully would become the first to benefit from this ground-breaking, big-animal dental technology.

Steenkamp anticipated that he might have to look for innovative solutions involving engineering and mechanics, so he had arranged for Dannie Burger and At von Wielligh, lecturers from the Department of Mechanical and Aeronautical Engineering at Pretoria University, to be present on the day, as was technician Jan Brand. As the operation progressed, Steenkamp and his team assessed the situation and modified the plan to fit what they found.

Two serious cracks were discovered in the outer shell of the dentine, and it became clear that the abscess was much deeper in the tooth than originally thought, and the bacteria causing the infection were migrating up the cracks. During the operation, the cracked tooth was held together by a clamp while Dr Steenkamp attempted to cut a thread in the dentine into which to screw the plug. Due to positioning problems the cutting of the thread proved very difficult. The team had to reassess their plans fast because they were already 80 minutes into the operation, which was starting to give cause for concern over Bully's welfare.

The problems and discoveries encountered during the operation combined to convince Steenkamp that a permanent, rather than a removable, plug should be fitted. The clock was ticking so a new plug had to be made quickly. The technicians cut a length of approximately 40 millimetres from one of the existing plugs and chamfered the front to ease insertion when implanting. PMMA (polymethyl methacrylate) bone cement was then used to bond the plug into position, so Bully now had a semi-permanent filling in his tooth. The nylon plug fitted with the PMMA bone cement would slowly grow out at the end of the tusk and gradually wear off. It was hoped that the procedure had permanently eliminated the abscess and saved the tusk.

When the patient weighs well over 4 tonnes and doesn't always do exactly as human handlers would like, constant, detailed observation is much more difficult than in other circumstances. Nevertheless, Bully was kept under a close watch, and as the weeks went by John and Jenny became confident the operation had been a success.

Bully didn't appear to have any discomfort or to be in pain and the possibility of playing with his chain was precluded by his never again being tethered.

During this period he had daily interactions not only with John and his handlers, but also with Jonathan, and appeared in several films and TV commercials. Apart from occasional mischievousness Bully was always kind, co-operative and easy to handle. Had he been in pain this would probably not have been the case and this added to the belief that his dental problems had been solved.

In April 2004 Dr Steenkamp was in the area and called in to check that Bully's tusk was growing. In the two and a half years since the last filling there had been measurable growth and Bully once again seemed to have a healthy tusk.

In July 2008 a filming requirement presented an opportunity to check that all was still OK with Bully's tusk (see previous chapter). Bully was anaesthetised for the filming of 'Wild at Heart' and vets discovered that the tusk had grown, and that there was no recurrence of the fracture.

Gerhard Steenkamp continues to develop the treatment he pioneered with Bully, but he will always have a very special place in his memories for being the first-ever recipient.

Despite cutting-edge dental technology, careful observation and changes to management methods, Bully's tusk problems were to recur in later years. It is a measure of what an extraordinary animal he is that, although he must have had severe toothache from time to time, his behaviour never gave it away, and he was rarely bad tempered or dangerous.

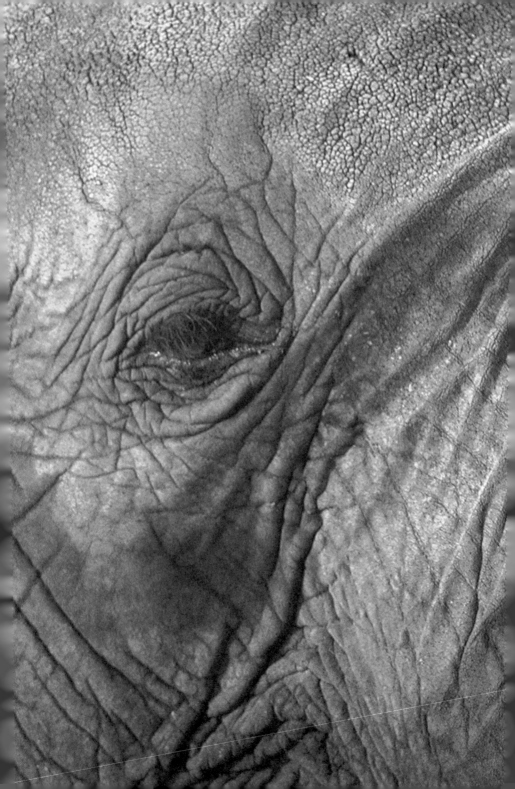

# 8

# INDUNA, 2003-2010

Two separate events occurred in 2003, both of which would have major impacts on Bully. The first was the retirement of Old Joe, and the second was the birth – far away – of a bull elephant which, in later life, would be called Induna, and would become Bully's best friend and constant companion.

It is impossible to overstate the importance of Old Joe in Bully's life. Bully was now a very powerful, boisterous, sometimes naughty teenager. The nearest thing in his life to a herd bull was a diminutive human. It is possible that memories of his elephant family were still present in the back of Bully's mind. It is certain that Old Joe had been in the front of his mind for the last 11 years, ever since his family was culled and Old Joe became, mother, father, best friend and mentor. A few stern words from Old Joe were all that was needed to stop Bully in his tracks if he was being silly or dangerous.

John thinks Old Joe was about 48 years old when Bully arrived. His had often been a hard, physical life and it had taken its toll. When working with animals many times bigger and stronger than him, speed and agility are often needed to avoid serious accidents. Old Joe would never have agreed but he simply wasn't as quick and fit as he used to be. Daily close contact with elephants, lions, cheetahs, leopards and others was a younger man's game. With regret and sadness John decided he had to let Old Joe go, and to retire him on a pension.

Although John was not sure of Old Joe's age he believed he was about 60. John hoped Old Joe still had many good years ahead of him, and felt he had more than earned his retirement on a good pension.

Old Joe died of Aids in 2008 but in his five years of retirement he was a regular visitor to Glen Afric. Bully was always happy to see him and was visibly upset when he left. As a highly intelligent creature, Bully knew how important Old Joe had been in his life, and felt a sense of loss just as a human would have done. John Brooker had a close relationship with Bully, and John's son Jonathan was a special friend too, but Old Joe had an almost mystical connection with the elephant; there is no doubt that his regular visits helped keep Bully stable during his early teenage years.

Induna was probably born in or near the Kruger National Park in 2003. He was sold at auction by the Park in 2005 or 2006, possibly to Ekland Safaris, which is a private game reserve involved in hunting in northern Limpopo.

The farm in northern Limpopo was home to Induna and his group for three years. Since their arrival and release on the farm they had largely been left alone to live as wild elephants. Here, Induna had the benefit of being with older elephants, which had adopted him and his group, and taught them elephant ways and language.

He had arrived on the farm with an older bull, which would later be named Gambo, and with two older cows, which became Amari and Shanti. Gambo played a dual role in Induna's life. He took the part of elder brother (indeed he may actually have been a brother), but in addition to being Induna's protector, he was also his persecutor. As far back as Induna could remember, Gambo had been the dominant figure in his life, either pushing him around or helping and leading him.

By the time he was sold to the farm in northern Limpopo, Induna had already developed a mistrust of humans. The only experiences he had were negative and often painful. He had been orphaned, darted, transported and sold at auction; then he had been released into a herd that had sometimes been hunted, and fear of humans as hunters was transmitted among the elephants.

Towards the end of 2007 the farm's owners decided they had to reduce their elephant numbers. The herd had increased in size, and the young elephants were growing up, which put unsustainable pressure on the farm.

The decision was taken to move some of the younger animals, and among those approached were Ian and Lisette Withers, who ran Elephants of Eden at Alexandria, near Port Alfred in the Eastern Cape. It was agreed the Withers would take four young elephants, and in February 2008 a team arrived to carry out the capture and transport of Induna, Gambo, Amari and Shanti.

This book would have contained a more detailed account of Induna and Bully's time at Elephants of Eden and the Knysna Elephant Park, based on taped interviews the author had with Mrs Lizette Withers (one of the owners), and with Dr Debbie Young and Sias van Rooyan who work at Knysna Elephant Park. The manuscript was sent to Elephants of Eden/Knysna Elephant Park for their comment and for fact checking; following this, permission for use of the material was withdrawn. As will be seen in later chapters, the NSPCA intends bringing a case, alleging cruelty and animal abuse, against Elephants of Eden, the Knysna Elephant Park and Mrs Withers. It is only fair to say that lawyers representing the Withers' operation felt that the author's analysis of the situation amounted to premature judgement. Other sources who, at their request, must remain unidentified, provided some background information, which is now included.

In his three-and-a-half years on the farm, Induna had roamed free and had had little contact with humans. His balanced and happy natural life in the wild was ended when he was struck by a dart containing the 'knock down' drug M99. He, Gambo, Amari and Shanti were all loaded into their own compartments behind the powerful transporter lorry that would take them south to Elephants of Eden. Already on board the transporter were four other young elephants, which were being moved from a farm near Musina to elephant trainers Rory and Lindie Hensman near Bella Bella.

After about 400 kilometres Induna and his group had a night stop at the Hensman farm where the other four elephants were dropped off. The next day Induna's group began the gruelling 1,150-kilometre drive to their new home at Elephants of Eden. Each animal would have been aware of the nearby presence of the others, from which they would have derived some comfort on their journey into uncertainty.

It was four very tired young elephants that were unloaded at Elephants of Eden after their 1,500-kilometre journey. Elephants arriving at facilities like Elephants of Eden and the Knysna Elephant Park are observed and assessed for behaviour and temperament in order to decide how best to manage them. Where animals are considered to be dangerous, handlers are not allowed to interact closely with them; those that are deemed less risky are able to interact with handlers, but staff work from behind protective barriers; and handlers react freely and regularly with trusted elephants, without protective measures.

Induna, Gambo, Amari, and Ashanti were wild when they arrived at Elephants of Eden. Other than when being transported and auctioned, they had never been held in stables and enclosures. Now they each had their own barred stable, and were let out into a larger enclosure (probably two hectares) during the day. This was likely because, although Elephants of Eden covered over 400 hectares, the elephants were not allowed to free roam because the reserve was not adequately fenced all around. For Induna and his group, this existence was a far cry from the freedom they had previously enjoyed.

Their ages are not known exactly, but when they arrived at Elephants of Eden, Gambo was probably nine or ten, Induna five or six, and Amari and Ashanti ten and eight years old, respectively.

Their ages and sizes probably made them ideal candidates to be trained to take human riders and to interact with the public. Training elephants to accept human riders is a controversial subject: many people believe it is wrong, as are the training methods employed. Ropes and chains are commonly used to make young elephants go down and eventually accept human passengers. Due to permission having been withdrawn, no discussion is allowed about the methods that were/are used at Elephants of Eden and Knysna Elephant Park. Within a few months Induna and Gambo had gone from being free-roaming young elephants living in a herd and being led, educated and supervised by older elephants, to being restrained, handled, roped, and kept in enclosures. Gambo was the stronger character, so Induna came to rely more and more on him, and his deep-seated fear and mistrust of humans probably increased.

Elephant trainers claim that, wherever possible, elephants are trained using positive rather than negative enforcement. Negative enforcement involves force, physical contact and possibly pain, whereas positive enforcement works on the reward principle. As stated earlier, comment on the training methods employed at Elephants of Eden and Knysna Elephant Park is not permitted here because permission to use this material has been withdrawn.

It seems likely that Elephants of Eden was largely a reception centre and training establishment, whereas the Withers' other operation, the Knysna Elephant Park, was where daily contact took place with the paying public. At the Knysna Park, elephants are lined up behind a barrier and the public can feed them with bits of fruit from buckets provided for the purpose. Elephants can be ridden, and people are photographed with them and allowed to touch and stroke them. Before all this can happen the elephants have to be trained, and sometimes things can go badly wrong.

The name Elephants of Eden suggests a safe haven or sanctuary and rehabilitation facility. However, it seems possible that its primary use was as a training and preparation centre to make elephants 'park friendly' or to prepare them for sale.

On 3 September 2008 Gambo killed Vanhuvmnwe Chinangama, an elephant handler from Zimbabwe. One version of events is that Gambo grabbed the handler through an electric fence and trampled him to death. Another is that Chinangama ventured into the elephant enclosure, which was against the rules. Horrific video footage taken soon after the incident would eventually be made public and would lead the NSPCA to consider bringing a case against the owners of Elephants of Eden/Knysna Elephant Park. The owners of Elephants of Eden/Knysna Elephant Park vigorously contest the NSPCA charges. Among other things, the video footage shows elephants, allegedly at Elephants of Eden, being trained using ropes, chains, electric prods and bull hooks. Gambo and Induna were among those in training at this time.

The Withers'/Elephants of Eden contention is that, following the death of Chinangama, he appeared in dreams to his handler colleagues and told them that if they didn't take revenge on Gambo he would haunt them. Induna probably got caught up in this violent retribution, and video footage (allegedly shot at Elephants of Eden) indicates elephants suffering horribly. Whether their abuse and injuries were the result of violent training, revenge taking, or both may be determined if there is a court case. Following the abuse incidents, Induna and Gambo were both taken to the Knysna Elephant Park so that their injuries could receive specialist treatment and they could be rehabilitated.

The killing of Chinangama by Gambo in 2008 wasn't the first such tragedy to occur at Elephants of Eden/Knysna Elephant Park. In June 2005, Harry, one of Knysna's first elephants, trampled a handler to death. Six years later in June 2011 the same elephant tossed his handler,

Arnold Ndzwanana, in the air, then trampled him. Arnold lived but had to have a leg amputated. Some say that the growing number of people being killed and injured by captive elephants around the world amounts to a rebellion by these animals. This is not inconceivable: during research for *Giant Steps*, three expert elephant handlers with many years' experience recounted incidents where elephants, clearly resentful of their treatment, had reacted violently towards the handler concerned.

The NSPCA's official, widely published comment on the matter was:

'The National Council of SPCAs (NSPCA) has laid animal cruelty charges against Elephants of Eden, the Knysna Elephant Park, their directors and management including Lizette Withers, in terms of the Animals Protection Act, 71 of 1962 for cruelty to elephants.

'This proved necessary after the NSPCA received horrific footage depicting the cruel and abusive training methods employed to control and train baby and young elephants for their future, captive lives in the elephant-based tourist industry.'

According to a press statement from Wendy Willson, the national NSPCA inspector, 'The footage shows elephant calves and juvenile elephants being chained, roped and stretched, shocked with electric cattle prods and hit with bull hooks – all methods used to force these gentle giants to submit to the will of their trainers and handlers.' She also said, 'The elephants show signs of crippling injuries with severely swollen legs and feet, debilitating abscesses and wounds resulting from the use of ropes, chains and bull hooks.'

Willson's interpretation of the footage and her opinion as to what happened is strongly contested by Withers and those at the Knysna Elephant Park. When the NSPCA High Court case proceeds, the court will decide on the guilt or innocence of the accused. Prior to this, in September 2015, the Grahamstown Director of Public Prosecutions decided not to proceed with the case and charges were dropped. The NSPCA, however, is still proceeding with its civil case in the High Court.

Once Induna and Gambo had been treated and their rehabilitation begun, they were returned to Elephants of Eden. Their lives now became a daily routine of being stabled at night, and let out into the elephant camps each day. Induna was a nervous and frightened young elephant, and it would be two years before a new, calming influence would enter his life.

At the time the below statement was issued, the NSPCA confirmed that they were proceeding against Elephants of Eden/Knysna Elephant Park in a Civil case in the High Court in Grahamstown. The case number is CAS 4234/2013 and at the time this book went to press the NSPCA were still waiting for a date for the case to be heard.

On 20 November 2015 the NSPCA issued the following statement:

# MEDIA STATEMENT
### ISSUED ON 20 November 2015
### CONTACT PERSON Isabel Wentzel
### (011 – 907 3590 or 082 575 0241)

## NSPCA GRIEVES FOR ELEPHANTS

In May 2014 the National Council of SPCAs (NSPCA) laid animal cruelty charges against Elephants of Eden, the Knysna Elephant Park, their directors and management in terms of the Animals Protection Act, 71 of 1962 for cruelty to elephants. This proved necessary after the NSPCA received horrific footage depicting the cruel and abusive training methods employed to control and train baby and young elephants for their future, captive lives in the elephant-based tourist industry.

Despite our efforts on behalf these elephants, Advocate J. C. Coetzee, the Director of Public Prosecutions : Grahamstown (in a letter dated 12 November 2015) confirmed to the NSPCA his decision not to prosecute the case, stating that he had not been persuaded that 'the "training methods" employed indeed constituted "cruel" treatment and/or caused "unnecessary" suffering to the elephants involved.'

'We are shocked and don't feel that justice has been served,' said Senior Inspector Isabel Wentzel – 'The facts have been disregarded, despite the factual evidence as well as the supporting evidence of national and international elephant specialists who confirmed the excessive and extensive physiological and psychological injuries suffered by the elephants. The elephants showed signs of severely swollen legs and feet, debilitating abscesses and wounds resulting from the abusive use of ropes, chains and bull hooks – injuries sustained at Elephants of Eden.'

The NSPCA remains opposed to the removal of elephants from the wild and 'taming' them for lifelong captivity. Since the Tuli elephant case (the NSPCA uncovered unacceptable training methods and laid criminal charges) which began at the end of 1997, the NSPCA has been calling upon our government to enforce stricter measures to protect elephants.

This protection has not materialised.

We grieve for our country's elephants.

Three knew exactly what to do at the birth of her baby.

# 9

# THREE, HANNA AND MARTY

By 1997 the only elephants left at Glen Afric from the original 1992 Kruger orphans were Bully, Three and Mopani. In 2002/2003 it was decided to sell Mopani and she went to Craig Saunders at the Knysna Elephant Sanctuary (not to be confused with the Knysna Elephant Park). For the next four years Bully and Three would be the only two elephants at the farm.

Musth is a Hindu word meaning 'mischievous' and is used to describe the change in behaviour among Indian bull elephants when their hormone levels rose. The temporal glands between the eye and the ear become swollen and secrete a clear, oily liquid, which runs down and stains the side of the face black. There is a dribble from the penis that also stains the insides of the legs black, and the greenish-yellow urine smells strongly of testosterone.

When Mopani left, Bully was 10 years old; about three years later he starting coming into musth, which usually occurs much earlier in captive or semi-captive bulls than in wild ones (usually in their twenties).

Females in the wild start coming into oestrus at about 11–12 years old, and generally prefer mating with older bulls, probably because older bulls are more experienced and less violent. Captive and semi-captive cows usually start coming into oestrus earlier, at about seven to eight years, which was the case with Three.

**97**

In the middle of 2007 Jenny started suspecting that Three might be pregnant. She bought a human pregnancy testing kit, got one of the grooms to catch some urine in a bottle, and dipped the litmus stick into it. The test showed positive. Various people pointed out that this could hardly be regarded as a conclusive test due to the differences between human and elephant hormones, both in type and levels, but Jenny knew Three was pregnant. Her suspicions were confirmed by an early morning call on 31 December, 2007 from the grooms who had arrived for work and found Three had given birth.

Jenny has moved fast many times in her life, but she thinks that the fastest she ever moved was in response to this call. She was at the elephant house barely five minutes later, and now there were three elephants. Bully's daughter had been born at around 6.30 a.m., and Bully was, rather comically, sitting on his backside in the next-door stable, observing events with an unconcerned, rather bemused air.

As a father, Bully was interested and perhaps confused, rather than, more conventionally, stressed and concerned. Telling the story eight years later, Jenny's obvious pleasure at the birth of the baby elephant had not diminished: 'We got there and she was all wet, shiny, pink, bloody and what have you'. Baby Hannah weighed between 80 and 100 kilograms and, as Three probably weighed over 2 tonnes, it was hardly surprising there had been no visible clues to her being pregnant. Although she was a very young mother, Three had known exactly what to do. She had been lying down when, soon after 2 a.m., she knew things were slowly starting to happen. She got up and stood until 4 a.m., and just after 6 started to move restlessly round her stable. Just before 6.30 a.m. she crouched and started pushing; and minutes later Hannah landed on the stable floor with a wet thump.

Jenny couldn't praise Three enough: 'She was brilliant, she allowed us to go in there, and help the baby stand, and take its first steps. I think

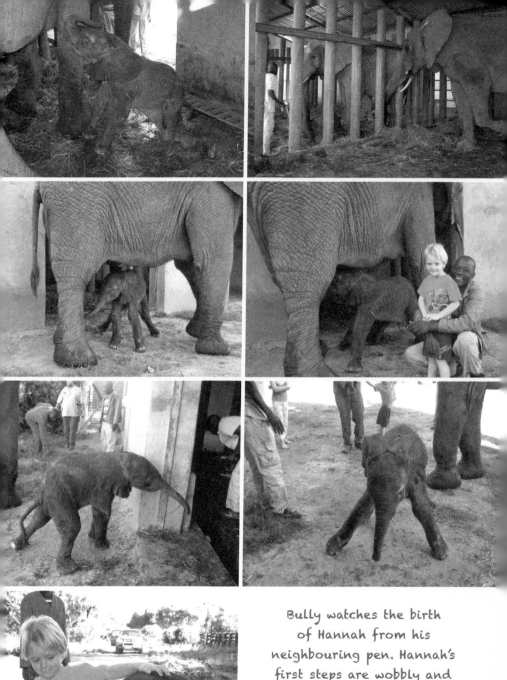

Bully watches the birth
of Hannah from his
neighbouring pen. Hannah's
first steps are wobbly and
uncertain, but Jonathan now
has a new young friend.

this was amazing as most animals don't normally allow you near their babies. The floor in the stable was a mess as the placenta was out and separated from the baby and on the floor, and there was amniotic fluid all over the place. We got them out onto dry ground, and within half an hour the baby was standing, and within an hour she was steady on her feet. The baby couldn't reach the teat and Three showed what a brilliant mum she was by going down on her elbows so the baby could reach.'

Bully had watched everything from his stable through the widely spaced bars that separated him from Three. He had watched the labour, the birth, the arrival of Jenny, Hannah's first steps, and Jenny taking Three and Hannah outside. If he was a proud father that day he didn't really show it. What he did show in the days and weeks that followed was that he was a hugely affectionate father who really appreciated his new daughter.

For the next two days Bully went out by himself while Three and Hannah stayed in. But from day three he could be seen proudly leading his family out into the bush each morning. It is probably wrong to relate human emotions to those of animals, but Bully and Three appeared to behave towards their baby very much as humans do towards their young. To all at Glen Afric, Bully, Three and Hannah were people, and Hannah's birth put a smile on every face on the farm.

Bully and Three may have been young and inexperienced, but imbedded instinct is strong and they were model parents. This was good because their parenting skills would soon be called upon to help another orphan.

Twenty-one days after Hannah was born the Brookers got a call from the Kruger Park where one of the rangers had found a new-born calf abandoned in the south near the Crocodile River. They were asked to take the orphan in the hope that Three would feed and rear it with Hannah. John was known to have successfully reared milk calves so if Three wouldn't feed the calf, hand-rearing was the fallback option. The next day Jenny picked up the tiny female elephant from a local airstrip and took her back to Glen Afric under the canopy at the back of her vehicle.

Hannah was 23 days old when her new companion arrived. No-one knew what Three's reaction would be; she might either reject the new calf or accept it. Three and Hannah had fully bonded, and together with Bully were a family unit. Within the structure of elephant herds orphans are cared for by relatives, but the little calf was not related, and, however tiny and helpless, was nevertheless an intruder.

The new baby, named Marty, was very hungry indeed by the time she was introduced to Three, who accepted her immediately; Bully now had an adopted daughter and Hannah had a new little sister. Four elephants now paraded daily out into the bush, with Bully leading the way. Jenny remembers, 'Three knew which was which, but she treated them exactly the same. Bully also treated them the same, but whether he knew which was which, I don't know; he probably did – elephants are very intelligent. She sometimes reprimanded them but they got away with a lot, they were naughty little babies, but completely captivating, it was impossible not to be in love with them. It was wonderful to watch them playing together, and we often used to guess at just how annoying Bully or Three would let them get before there would be a gentle reprimand.'

Although still relatively young, Bully was now in every sense a developing bull elephant, but with no herd bull to guide his behaviour, and not even Old Joe, who by now was dead. He was coming into musth, was a father, and he knew he was the dominant creature in his surroundings: he was changing and growing up. Glen Afric, meanwhile, was evolving into a successful, multi-faceted commercial business. The two were on a collision course, and over the next two years several incidents would indicate that the situation was becoming untenable, and that change was inevitable.

Three now had two new babies, and Hannah a new baby sister. They were mischievous little babies but completely captivating and impossible not to love.

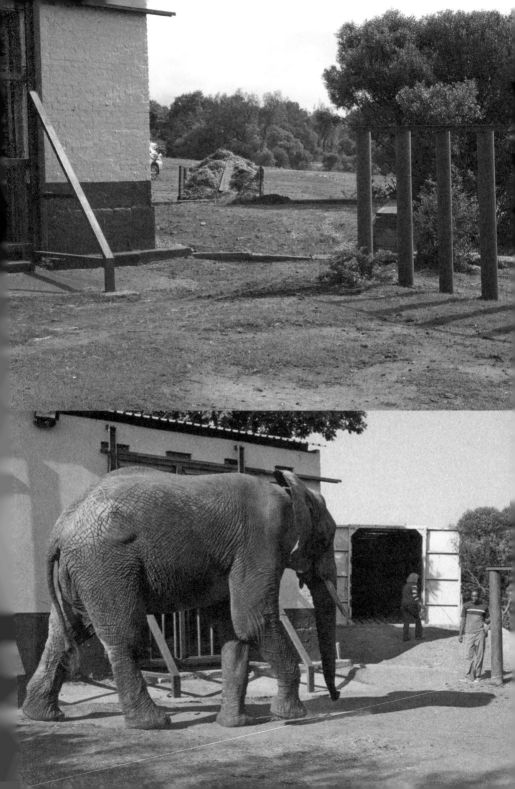

# 10

# JONATHAN SAYS GOODBYE

When Bully and the other calves had first arrived at what was then known as the Brooker Farm, it was used as a quarantine station and holding area for various game species. Apart from the Brooker house and the quarantine sheds, there were very few buildings and the elephants wandered off by themselves into the bush every morning and returned in the evening.

What had been a large, open area with few buildings, slowly changed as film set structures went up, roads were built, and a lodge for visitors was constructed.

The development of Glen Afric led to new routines and restrictions that Bully had not had to contend with before. As activity and traffic on the farm increased, he was tempted to interact: he played with a few cars, tried to re-design a building or two, and chased people on a couple of occasions. John and Jenny Brooker insist that Bully's behaviour was never malicious, he was just having fun; but what is fun to a teenage bull elephant could be alarming and dangerous to any humans involved who weren't familiar with him.

A few months after the birth of Hannah a mistake by a handler caused Bully to knock him over. Three was in season and Bully was trying to mate with her. The two calves were underneath Three, and the handlers, fearing the calves would come to harm, tried to get them out. This interference with mating prompted Bully, using his trunk, to send one of the handlers flying. The Brookers had warned their staff never to interfere when animals are mating: the calves would have been safe because Three would not have let anything happen to them.

No harm had come to the handlers other than bruises all around; bruised bodies, bruised egos and bruised confidence. However, this incident was a watershed, and the Brookers started thinking the unthinkable – another home would have to be found for Bully. Before coming to this conclusion all the options were examined as John and Jenny knew that re-homing Bully would not only leave a massive hole at Glen Afric, it would also break Jonathan's heart. Among other solutions, they considered increased restrictive management and the use of testosterone blockers: but in the end, re-homing Bully became inevitable. Jenny Brooker explained: 'He needed space, and he needed to be able to just roam and be an elephant. Clearly he couldn't be returned to the wild so we looked for the next best thing. Lisette Withers told us about her 1,000-hectare Elephants of Eden facility, and said she had some females there that Bully could be released with.'

The offer by Lisette to take Bully presented the ideal solution. A stage payment price was agreed and a contract was signed. Bully would soon be on his way south to meet Induna.

In September 2010 Jonathan was seven years old. For several weeks he had known he was going to lose his best friend. He lay awake at night praying that things would change and Bully would stay. He talked to him and told him to behave because he thought that if there were no more incidents, his parents might change their minds.

The date for Bully's move was set for 25 September, 2010 and, as the day approached, the ache in Jonathan's heart and the empty feeling in his stomach got bigger. He knew he had to be brave. He didn't want Bully or his parents to see him cry. But how do you lose your best friend, how do you say goodbye without crying? He couldn't remember a day of his life without Bully. When he was a toddler the elephants walked past the house every day and Jonathan went with them and the handlers into the bush. While still in nappies he ran around between Bully's legs and the elephant would gently pick him up with his trunk. Later, the two played games together, and Jonathan would give Bully fruit and titbits to eat.

When Bully's broken tusk was painful, Jonathan sensed it and talked to him, and Bully's soft rumblings in response showed his gratitude for Jonathan's concern. And so the extraordinary bond between them deepened.

Now Bully was going away forever and Jonathan struggled with the enormity of it. The decision had been made with regret, for good reasons, and in Bully's best interests, and while Jonathan knew this, he also wished there were another way.

When the day arrived, straight after breakfast Jonathan ran to the elephant house, slid through the bars and sat with Bully. He didn't speak but Bully did in deep gentle rumbles as he touched the little boy with his trunk. Hannah and Marty were now three years old and were with their mother in the next-door stable. The elephants picked up Jonathan's mood and shared his silent sadness.

They all heard the transporter lorry arrive and position itself at the special loading ramp John had built. Jonathan heard his parents' voices and that of the vet above the throb of the transporter's idling engine. The elephant handlers arrived and let Three, Hannah and Marty out for their day in the bush. They knew something was happening and didn't want to leave Bully. Their trunks snaked through the bars of his stable to touch him and seek reassurance. The handlers called them and they followed, but there was no joy in going out into the bush that day.

The vet sent by Lisette Withers slightly sedated Bully as it was hoped this would make it easier to load him. In the end it took four hours to get him into the transporter, and Jenny is convinced that the sedation actually made loading more difficult, and that had he not been sedated he would have walked straight up the ramp.

Bully may still have had faint memories of a life before Glen Afric, but the Brookers' farm, the Brooker family, Old Joe, and more recently his elephant family of Three, Hannah and Marty were his whole life and now he sensed he was leaving it behind. He would not load: he didn't resist violently, but he was stubborn, and confused by the sedative.

Three, Hannah and Marty reappeared and now they realised that Bully was leaving. They crowded around him and touched him with their trunks, and Three and Bully spoke to each other with their deep, soft rumbles. The handlers took the other elephants away again, and efforts to load Bully continued. Bully had always done what John asked of him, and today he didn't not do what was asked of him, he simply did nothing. He either stood immobile or backed slowly away. All his favourite treats and rewards were tried, but even oranges and carrots didn't interest him.

Jonathan sat on the ground with his back against the wall of the elephant house and with his knees drawn up under his chin. He struggled to stop his lower lip trembling and held back the tears. Bully looked sad and uncertain and Jonathan hated watching his friend looking so unhappy. He stood up, his chin jutted forward in determination, his lower lip became firm, and he walked towards Bully who was rooted to the ground at the end of the ramp.

'Come on Bully, you can do it', and he walked up behind Bully and underneath him and pushed behind one of his front legs. Bully didn't respond, and Jonathan walked a few steps up the ramp. 'Come on Bully you can do it, I know you can do it.' Bully raised his trunk, saluted his little friend and took a few steps towards him, not giant steps but small, shuffling, almost uncertain steps.

Slowly, metre by metre, Jonathan coaxed Bully up the ramp and into the big transporter. Bully was quickly secured by Lucas the handler, who would go with him to settle him into Elephants of Eden.

Jonathan trudged slowly away towards the house on the longest walk of his life. He heard the lorry's engine start, and couldn't look back but spoke through his tears. 'Goodbye Bully, I'll always love you, and I'll come and find you one day.' For the second time in his life, Bully had lost his whole family, and once again he struggled with a deep sense of grief and loss.

Until Jonathon came to help, Bully wouldn't go up the ramp.

Bully had gone, but daily life at Glen Afric for Three, Hannah and Marty went on as before.

# 11

# ELEPHANTS OF EDEN

Many hours after having left Glen Afric the transporter arrived at Elephants of Eden. By then, Bully was a tired, worried, and possibly frightened elephant. He was also in pain as his tusk had cracked again and another abscess was forming. When Lucas unloaded Bully and put him into a pen he knew that all was not well. The sedation had worn off several hours ago, and Bully was not only wide awake, he also seemed wary and on his guard. Lucas understood why but had not seen this behaviour before: Bully had immediately sensed that his new home was a far cry from the familiar, relaxed and laid-back life he had known for the last 18 years at Glen Afric.

As has been described earlier with Induna's group, on arrival Bully's behaviour and temperament would have been assessed to decide on a management system. He was not considered to be an elephant with which unprotected interaction was appropriate. At Glen Africa a small boy happily ran around underneath him and between his legs, now he was in a very different management regime.

After a few days Lucas said goodbye to Bully and returned to Glen Afric. He hoped Bully would be alright but wasn't altogether sure, and told the Brookers of his misgivings. John and Jenny had always expected there would be settling-in problems; but they trusted that Bully would soon be free-roaming with females in 1,000 hectares of open bush.

Soon after arriving at Elephants of Eden, it was noticed that the shorter of Bully's tusks was loose. Dr Gerhard Steenkamp was called and together with Dr Brendan Tindall carried out a procedure on 16 December, 2010. Bully had to be completely anaesthetised for the examination, during which Dr Steenkamp confirmed that the tusk was loose and so decided to extract it. Bully added another 'first' to his ever-growing list when he became the first elephant on record to have a tusk extracted using golf-cart technology! Dr Steenkamp explained: 'The normal way of extraction is piece by

At the Knysna Elephant Park the public can interact with the elephants.

piece, but with Bully's tusk, because it was loose, and because it wasn't hollow on the inside anymore, I used the winch from a little golf cart which we put around the tusk to extract it. Just a gentle traction and it came out. Bully was the first; more recently I did a similar extraction in Poland using the experience I initially had with Bully.'

When extracting the tusk Dr Steenkamp also found loose bits of tusk material called pearls that had broken off. Bully had been having problems with his tusk for over 11 years and during this period would often have been in great pain. He was now an elephant with only one tusk but, for the first time in many years, lived in a pain-free world.

The final episode in the tusk saga was in April 2011 when Dr Steenkamp came to do a follow-up examination. There was still puss coming from the empty socket so he scoped the empty alveolus where the tusk had been. He found the source of the continuing infection was a small fragment of ivory that was still present. After this last piece of ivory had been removed, Bully healed rapidly and successfully. This was the first time Steenkamp had used an endoscope purpose-built for elephant vasectomies in the alveolus of a tusk.

By the time Bully arrived at Elephants of Eden, Induna and Gambo had returned from their veterinary and rehabilitation treatment at the Knysna Elephant Park. It was decided to put Bully, Induna and Gambo together as a bachelor group, both in terms of stabling them next door to each other and letting them share the same camp each day. It was a good decision, and particularly so for Bully and Induna. Gambo appeared to have come through the alleged cruelty and abuse episode better than Induna. He was older, bigger and a stronger character. Induna was led by Gambo but was also bullied by him, and was never relaxed when humans were around him.

On their arrival at Elephants of Eden, the elephants'
behaviour and temperament would have been assessed.

Bully and Induna soon developed a strong bond and Gambo's influence over Induna decreased markedly. Apart from his tusk problems, and being moved to the more restricted regime at Elephants of Eden, Bully had always been a happy soul. In the words of Jonathan Brooker, Bully was 'a calm, kind and generous elephant', and these qualities were exactly what were needed to bring stability and reassurance into Induna's troubled life.

In their small camp there would have been a drinking waterhole, a mud wallow and a tree, and because relatively small camps don't provide much space for three elephants, they amused themselves playing for most of the day when they weren't feeding. Bully was now clearly the dominant animal, and he always defended Induna if Gambo picked on him.

Although Bully had left his human and elephant families behind at Glen Afric, and had keenly felt the loss, he now had his little bachelor group of Induna and Gambo; and Induna, in particular, helped fill the void.

Bully's life had started with the cull that left him an orphan, and it is likely that Induna's had started in much the same way. But, whereas Bully's 19 years had mostly been happy ones, Induna's life of half that span had largely been one of upheaval, change, uncertainty, bullying and, allegedly, cruelty and abuse.

Bully, Induna and Gambo were regarded as troubled elephants at Elephants of Eden. Prior to his tusk removal, Bully had wrecked his pen and done other damage. He had been placed in the 'hands off' management category for elephants that were considered to be dangerous. Someone who worked at Elephants of Eden at the time reported that it had been decided to sell Bully because they couldn't manage him and probably considered him untrainable.

Induna was a very wary, troubled elephant; and he would also be difficult to train.

Inverdoorn is the
largest of the three private
game reserves close to Cape Town.

# 12

# INVERDOORN

he Inverdoorn private game reserve lies in the Tankwa Karoo, only two-and-a-half hours by road from Cape Town. Most of the land was previously a fruit farm before it was bought by Jean-Michel and Cathy Vergnaud in 1994. The Vergnauds wanted to own a piece of Africa and return it to its original state. They love wildlife and so started acquiring and releasing animals. The bush slowly started to re-establish itself, and the evolution of Inverdoorn from fruit farm to game reserve had begun.

With free-roaming cheetahs living naturally at Inverdoorn, it is the only game reserve close to Cape Town where visitors can see large predatory cats living genuinely wild lives. The total reserve covers 10,000 hectares, but the fenced safari area is about half that. Sadly, the presence of two bordering roads, and the current poaching scourge, make it impossible for the Vergnauds to utilise the whole of the area as part of the reserve.

When Jean-Michel and Cathy Vergnaud had first told their son Damian that they were spending all their retirement money to buy an arid, failed fruit farm, his reaction was: 'You are crazy!' However, as time went on Damian became more involved in the reserve until his passion for Inverdoorn matched that of his parents. By 2011 Jean-Michel and Cathy had handed over most of the running of the reserve to Damian, who continued the transformation from fruit farm to acclaimed game reserve. Lions, hippos, rhinos, giraffe, zebra, wildebeest, meerkats, kudu, eland, blesbok, buffalo, lechwe, cheetahs, bat-eared foxes, Cape foxes, springbok and others are all regularly seen on game drives; and while leopards are an elusive rarity, there is often evidence of their presence.

Inverdoorn is the largest of the three private game reserves close to Cape Town. The others are Aquila, near Touws River, and Fairy Glen, which is just outside Worcester. Although the Vergnaud's reserve was the biggest and had the most species and the largest number of animals, it did not have the Big Five – lion, leopard, elephant, buffalo and rhino – something both Fairy Glen and Aquila could boast having. Damian knew that to retain his pre-eminent position he had to have the Big Five too.

Damian Vergnaud was born in the Ivory Coast in 1973. Jean-Michel was a road architect and mechanical engineer, and Cathy and her young son spent much time in the jungle with him. When Damian was nine years old he was sent to France for his education and then took up music; he started out as a jazz pianist, and ended up making electronic music that earned him gold discs. His African birth and childhood meant, however, that the continent was in his blood and never far from his thoughts. He returned permanently in 2003, at the age of 30, and joined his parents.

Damian's background in the entertainment industry, his grasp of the modern IT world and his passion for Africa, combined with the experience gained from his parents, led to Inverdoorn becoming the leader in its field in the Western Cape, and to its making notable contributions to wildlife conservation.

Damian didn't simply want to add elephants to Inverdoorn and so 'have the Big Five'. He also wanted to make sure that he had the right number of elephants for the size of the reserve, that they could be released and roam free as much as possible, that issues with other species wouldn't cause problems, and that their feed could be supplemented properly. He wanted their boma area to be as large as possible; but, above all, he wanted to give a good home to elephants that needed it.

The owners of captive elephants in South Africa are mostly known to each other, and there are only a few possible sources for private reserves like Inverdoorn. Damian put the word out that he was looking to acquire elephants: soon he was offered three wild females from the Kruger Park, and at about the same time, he heard about Bully and Induna. He was told that Bully had had a sad life and needed a new chance. This was hardly true because, for most of the time, Bully had had anything but a sad life for a captive elephant. Damian was told lots of stories about Bully's troubled past, but they were largely untrue. Bully was depicted as being very dangerous, and his 'history' included some horrific incidents, including that he had killed an actor on a film set – as it turned out, a case of wrong elephant ID. Little was said about Induna, possibly because of the 2008 abuse after Gambo had killed a handler.

Instead of putting Damian off, the horror stories merely sharpened his interest and he went to see Bully and Induna for himself. As Damian put it, 'When I went to meet Bully, his condition was a disaster, he was very skinny, and was very distant. I felt a connection with Bully straight away. I spent a few hours with him, he came to the fence and I fed him a little.'

Damian's parents also went to see Bully and they all agreed they would take him. One of the conditions of sale was that Induna would go with Bully. This was good for both elephants as it would lessen the trauma of being moved and then re-adjusting to a new environment. Initially, Elephants of Eden tried to interest Damian in taking Gambo as well, but he didn't have the financial resources for all three.

Before Inverdoorn would be able to accommodate two of the worlds' largest mammals there was a lot of preparation to be done. By law, elephant camps have to be at least two hectares in size; and to hold elephants securely, the whole camp area had to be enclosed by a robust, elephant-proof fence or boma wall. Within the camp, mud baths and a waterhole had to be provided. The purchase price of Bully and Induna was only the beginning, and by the time they arrived at Inverdoorn the investment ran into millions. The original motivation had been to acquire elephants to make up the Big Five and so be able to compete with Aquila and Fairy Glen. However, once he had met Bully and Induna, Damian's obsession was with giving them back their freedom, and financial considerations became almost secondary.

As soon as he had decided to acquire elephants Damian had started to plan preparations. Building elephant camps is simply a matter of construction, which Damian would deal with when the time came. What concerned him more was finding someone to look after his elephants; not only someone he could trust, and was proven to be competent, but also someone who showed he had a special connection with the animals.

Two years before Bully and Induna arrived at Inverdoorn, Damian had visited the Addo Elephant National Park near Port Elizabeth. Working there at the time was a Zimbabwean called Mishak. There had been an instant rapport between them and now, casting his mind back, Damian felt that he had identified his man. He had watched Mishak in action, working with Addo elephants, and had made discreet enquiries with his current employers to check his background and previous employment. Before he left Addo, Damian asked Mishak for his contact details and said he would be in touch. One year later Mishak had almost forgotten about his meeting with Damian when he received a message. Damian was telling him that preparations for the arrival of elephants was now under way, and was offering him a job. Mishak arrived at the reserve several months before Bully and Induna and assisted with getting everything ready.

It had been over 200 years since elephants had last trodden the Tankwa Karoo. The pieces of the jigsaw puzzle that would show Bully and Induna taking giant steps back to an old elephant stomping ground – and to freedom – were falling into place.

Damian wanted someone who showed he had a special connection with the elephants – Mishak had that connection.

Mishak believes he 'feels' elephants
and that they 'feel' him.

# 13

# THE ELEPHANT WHISPERER

ishak Mbaur is one of four Zimbabwean brothers, all of whom work with elephants. Most of those working with captive elephants in South Africa are from Zimbabwe, where elephant-back safaris were pioneered.

Mishak was 18 years old and had been away looking for work. He was on the road walking home before Christmas when a car stopped beside him. At first he thought he was being given a lift, but the driver, another Zimbabwean, called Clem Coetzee, knew Mishak and had stopped to offer him a job, not a lift. At that time Mishak's English was not good, and he wasn't sure what Coetzee was saying but he heard the word 'job', and jumped into the vehicle.

Unbeknown to Mishak, Coetzee had also hired his brother Davison earlier the same day, and they were to be trained to work with elephants as handlers and trainers. First they had to learn all about the animals, and Coetzee sent them away to trainers Rory and Lindie Hensman to get their elephant education.

Six months later they returned, and with Coetzee they went to Gonarezhou National Park where they were shown a group of elephants, and told to choose one each with which to work. Mishak chose a female and Davison chose a male. The job was to train them for people to ride, and the brothers were so good at it that they had trained their first two elephants in less than six months. More elephants followed and Mishak believes that in this phase of his career, he was involved in the training of about 20 elephants. Their mother was unhappy having two of her sons working with elephants. However, Mishak and Davison both showed a real aptitude for the work, and eventually their two younger brothers would also become elephant handlers.

The world of captive-elephant owners and trainers is small and, because Mishak and Davison had made names for themselves, they were contacted by Lente Roode and offered jobs at the Kapama Game Reserve in Limpopo. They worked there for eight years, after which Mishak went to work at the Addo Elephant National Park near Port Elizabeth in the Eastern Cape. Three years later he moved to Inverdoorn to join Damian.

Mishak considers that when Coetzee offered him his first job, he gave him a great gift. He also believes that working with elephants is an honour and a privilege. Mishak wasn't only given a gift, he also possesses one: the gift of being able to relate to his elephants and understand them. He was taught how to train elephants using ropes and chains, but is adamant that the Hensman operation never involved cruelty. The training went at the pace the elephants dictated, with some learning faster than others and so being trained more quickly. Ropes were training aids rather than instruments of force, and Mishak believes that, because of the way he relates to elephants, he can train them without any ropes or chains as long as he is given enough time. He claims to be able to train an average elephant to accept human riders within eight months – without using any ropes or chains.

Mishak explains that, very early on, after having met an elephant for the first time, he makes his connections with the animal. These connections are different with each animal, and come about after he has assessed and spoken with the elephant and 'felt' it. He believes he 'feels' elephants and that they 'feel' him. There is no doubt that some humans get on better with animals than others do. Old Joe had an almost mystical way of connecting with animals, and Mishak has a similar ability with elephants.

We know nothing about how elephants and other animals 'see' humans and assess us as individuals; that they do this is beyond doubt. It is the only explanation why, on a first meeting, animals respond favourably to some people, but not to others. Do we have some sort of aura that is invisible to us but can be seen or sensed by animals? If so, Mishak's aura signals to his elephants that he is on their side and can be trusted.

By the time Mishak met Bully and Induna, the elephant handler had already heard much about them, and it was largely negative. Rumours abounded about their having killed people, destroyed pens and enclosures, and being 'hands off' because they were too dangerous and difficult to handle.

At his first meeting with Bully, however, Mishak knew instinctively that they would be friends because Bully had an open, kind and honest face.

In contrast, Induna's face told of problems, mistrust, and fear. But Mishak sensed that Induna was not bad, it would just take a long time to gain his trust and stop him from being fearful and wary around people. Mishak knew that Bully was the key figure in Induna's life, and that Bully would help him to help Induna. By building a bond with Bully, Mishak would also slowly start to get close to, and be trusted by Induna. Quite simply, Bully would signal to Induna that 'this man is OK'.

In his earlier life on the Brookers' farm, Bully had trusted and relied on Old Joe, John and Jonathan. Now he was about to meet two new human kindred spirits at Inverdoorn – Damian and his elephant whisperer.

Mishak knew they would be friends because Bully had an open, kind and honest face.

All at the
reserve eagerly awaited
the arrival of the elephants.

# 14

# GIANT STEPS

The price and terms were agreed and the date was set for Bully and Induna to move to their new home. The new elephant camp at Inverdoorn had long been finished and equipped, and Damian, Mishak and everyone at the reserve eagerly awaited the arrival of the elephants.

Sadly, the loading and transportation process at Elephants of Eden cannot be described because, as stated, permission to use this material has been withdrawn. However, we know from other sources that by midday Bully and Induna were loaded and on their way to their new home in the Western Cape.

There were regular stops when the elephants were checked, and they had food and water all the way. Neither animal was a stranger to being transported, and they travelled well and were relatively stress-free.

Inverdoorn is approached on an untarred, graded road, so arrivals are dusty and noisy at any time of the day. In the still of the Karoo night the truck's approach was heard a very long time before it finally turned off the road and into the reserve.

Bully didn't need any encouragement: he left the huge travelling crate as soon as it was opened and walked into his new boma as if he had always lived there. And, wherever Bully led, Induna followed. Within an hour of their arrival, both elephants were in the boma and, after having conducted a thorough inspection, were eating lucerne and pieces of fruit.

Damian knew exactly what he wanted for his elephants. It was the same thing that he treasures most in his own life, and thinks is one of the most important things any human or animal can possess – freedom. He believed that Bully and Induna would now be as free as captive-raised elephants ever could be, with over 4,500 hectares in which to roam. They would find dammed water areas containing hippo, would meet many game species also roaming free, including buffalo and rhino, and would encounter a variety of vegetation and trees. Time would be needed to give them the confidence to take the necessary steps on their journey to living as semi-wild elephants.

The elephant camp at Inverdoorn would hold Bully and Induna during a familiarisation period prior to their release. A lot of thought had gone into making it as natural as possible, and it truly was a five-star elephant boma. It had trees in it and was also shaded by other trees outside the stockade fence. There was a drinking hole, mud wallow, and many places in the fence where people and elephants could interact.

Damian was keen to get the elephants released onto the reserve as soon as possible, but he is also a professional and a pragmatist. He knew that before the gate could be opened and the elephants released, there would have to be a period of assessment, familiarisation and planning.

Handlers and other staff from Elephants of Eden stayed and observed Bully and Induna for a few days, and then left. Damian and Mishak fed them fruit and other treats through the fence, and often entered the boma for free contact.

Neither Damian nor Mishak felt intimidated or threatened by the 'dangerous' elephant Bully was reputed to be. Bully quickly recognised that his life had changed and responded positively. Induna was different and from the outset it was obvious that it would take a long time to cure him of his mistrust of humans, which was so deeply engrained.

In the Zulu language the word 'Induna' or 'Nduna' means 'chief', and for two reasons Damian decided to modify Induna's name by abbreviating it to just 'Duna'. Firstly, on a symbolic level, Damian believed that a new name would herald a fresh start for the elephant; and secondly, he has a dislike of words like 'chief', so Induna became simply 'Duna' to all those in his new life.

Damian being interviewed by Expresso TV
prior to Bully and Duna's release.

The giant steps of elephants had not graced the Tankwa Karoo for over 200 years, so Damian believed that the day of their release onto the reserve to begin their semi-wild lives was significant and newsworthy. He planned to involve the media, whose attention would also help spread the word that Inverdoorn was now home to the Big Five.

Before the elephants were released there was a process of introduction to get them used to the idea of being able to roam free. Bully had roamed free over Glen Afric's 750 hectares, but he would now have an area six times that size, and it was four-and-a-half years since Duna had been anywhere bigger than in an elephant camp.

An electric fence was erected around the boma so that when the elephants were let out they wouldn't be able to go too far. Every couple of days the fence was moved back to give them a larger area. In this way, the elephants slowly became accustomed to their new freedom and their new surroundings. This gradual process also enabled Damian and the staff to study the impact the elephants were having on the trees and bushes within the boma, and to observe their behavioural traits.

Bully led the way each day and Duna followed, but he always stayed within a few metres of Bully as if frightened to stray too far from his protector. In spite of Duna's wariness of people, confidence gradually grew on both sides, and Damian decided on a date when the media would be invited to watch Bully and Duna be given the freedom of the whole reserve.

The sun was just up when a TV news crew and various journalists and photographers climbed into the waiting vehicles to be taken to witness Bully and Duna take their first, giant steps to a new life of semi-wild freedom. They could be seen behind the sturdy stockade fencing as they responded to Damian and Mishak's calls and moved towards the enormous, black, solid steel door that would open for them in a few minutes.

The opening of the door and the emergence of the elephants would mark several triumphs: elephants were returning to the Tankwa Karoo; Inverdoorn had become a Big Five game reserve; and the Vergnaud family's dream had come true – together, they had returned a small piece of Africa to its natural state. Finally, and most importantly, were the triumphs of Bully and Duna: they had survived being orphaned after their families were culled, and had endured losing friends, being transported over vast distances, being chained and restricted in small camps and subjected to the many indignities of life in captivity. In addition, Bully had suffered from recurring severe toothache.

Camera lenses were trained on the door so that they were ready to

Bully strides to freedom ...

record the moment of Bully and Duna's release. Bully didn't disappoint; it was almost as if he sensed he was back in front of the camera. Mishak slid the door back on its rollers, and Bully strode confidently out, completely ignoring the chatter and the clicking of cameras that signalled human attention; with Duna trailing him, he walked straight past the press and TV personnel, who were watching from behind the safety of an electrified fence. Bully was huge, majestic and proud, and as the elephants moved into the shrubbery and acacias both were soon lost to view.

Later, back at the Inverdoorn game lodge, there was an impromptu gathering of the media and the reserve staff. The smiles and excited chatter made it clear that everyone knew they had witnessed something very special.

At the time of Bully and Duna's release, elephant poaching for ivory was once again gathering pace. While these two elephants could now enjoy the rest of their lives living in semi-wild safety, sadly their cousins in other parts of Africa were not as lucky. In the next few years, poaching would grow to a point where one elephant was being killed by poachers every 15–20 minutes.

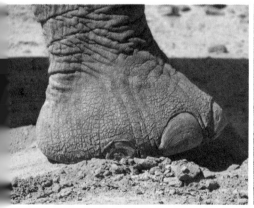

*... and makes an immediate impression.*

137

The giant steps
of elephants
had not graced the
Tankwa Karoo for
over 200 years.

Duna sprays dust all over his back.

# 15

# LIVING FREE

There are two large, concrete drinking holes in the centre of the Inverdoorn reserve, and this is also where, at certain times of the year, lucerne hay and other food is put down to supplement the diet of the grazing animals. Zebra, wildebeest, rhino, springbok, buffalo and many others often congregate at the waterhole in a happy mix of species.

Bully and Duna first visited the waterhole on their second day of full release, and many of the animals on the reserve were still unaware of their presence. As the elephants approached, sleeping animals woke, and those that were drinking and eating raised their heads and turned to watch the unaccustomed spectacle.

Like a huge galleon under full sail, Bully flapped his ears; and by his side, Duna, like a small escort vessel, took faster steps to keep up with him. As if by right, and as if he had always been there, Bully walked straight up to the waterhole and drank deeply. All the animals made way for him and Duna, and even the buffaloes moved off a short distance and then watched the elephants through sleepy eyes.

Bully and Duna snuffled around in the hay, ate a little, and then Duna used his trunk to spray dust all over his back. The other animals started to drift back to the waterhole and the remaining hay but, until Bully and Duna moved off, they gave them a wide berth.

Once they had finished at the waterhole, Bully continued his inspection of his new realm. Like a king saying goodbye to his subjects, he raised his trunk as he left the waterhole, and Duna hurried after him.

The Tankwa Karoo
is a land of extremes.

The Tankwa Karoo is a land of extremes. The summer temperature can reach 40°C degrees, and the searing heat dries out the land and ensures that the animals spend much of their day sleeping in the shade. In winter there is often snow on the higher of the surrounding mountains, and temperatures can get close to freezing.

Whether summer or winter, however, Bully and Duna's day always starts with the arrival of Mishak bringing breakfast. He unlatches the steel door, and when Bully is ready, he pushes it open and sets off for the day. At first, Duna followed Bully as soon as he left the boma, and always stayed close to him as they peacefully browsed and grazed. With time, Duna's confidence has grown and he no longer needs to be constantly close to Bully. They are often to be seen some distance apart, and sometimes make their way back to the boma separately.

Bully grew up having the run of Glen Afric and in the evening he always returned voluntarily to the elephant house. He has carried on this habit at Inverdoorn and returns to the boma each night without needing to be called or led. The evening feed that awaits him and his friend is an incentive to return, as are the fruit treats that Mishak produces.

When fully grown, Bully will be a very large and majestic bull, and were it not for the loss of one tusk, he would be an impressive 'tusker', like his father. A crucial aspect of Bully and Duna's management is to prevent them from coming into musth, and possibly being dangerous to their handlers and to tourists visiting the reserve. To counter the onset of this periodic state, testosterone-blocking drugs are used – a compromise that allows the elephants to enjoy their new freedom unfettered. These drugs are administered by the vet to avoid Bully or Duna developing negative associations towards Damian, Mishak, or other handlers.

Since their release, Bully and Duna, together with the wild cheetahs, have become the leading attractions at Inverdoorn. Cries ring out of 'Look, look, an elephant!' – there's no hiding the excitement in the voice of a visiting child as she spots Duna coming towards the safari vehicle. The ranger pulls slightly off the track to let Duna through, and the elephant pads quietly past the vehicle, only feet away from the tourists. Engrossed in watching Duna, they haven't seen Bully approaching from the other side. Suddenly he looms. He is almost twice Duna's size, and casts a huge shadow as he crosses the track in front of the vehicle and moves off towards some acacia trees. The astonished child almost forgets to breathe; this will forever remain one of the most magical moments of her young life.

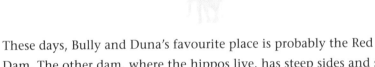

These days, Bully and Duna's favourite place is probably the Red Dam. The other dam, where the hippos live, has steep sides and so entry is more difficult. The Red Dam has gently sloping sides, and the easy walk into deeper water makes it ideal for elephants. It is about two kilometres from their boma and is often where they first head in the morning. The two elephants have been close friends for many years, so now they don't 'attack' play-time with quite the same energy as they did when they first met, when Duna was only seven or eight. But they still enjoy splashing, play-fighting, spraying water, swimming, mud-bathing and all the other pleasures of being elephants in water – to the full!

Damian often spends time with his elephants. He doesn't have to talk to them, get close, interact or do anything other than sit and watch the animals to which he gave the best gift he could: the priceless gift of freedom.

# PART TWO

# 16

# ELEPHANTS IN CAPTIVITY

lephants have been used by humans for centuries. In the Second Punic War (218–201 BC) Hannibal famously used elephants to help get his army across the Pyrenees and the Alps when he invaded Italy. In the long march, 38,000 infantry soldiers, 8,000 cavalry, and 38 elephants were used; sadly, few of the elephants survived the harsh Alpine conditions. Wherever they occur in Asia, elephants have been used as working animals; their size and strength make them ideal for transporting people and equipment.

In recent years, however, keeping wild animals in captivity has become an increasingly hotly debated issue, not least in respect of elephants. These huge mammals differ from other animals trained to serve humans: they are generally accepted as being more intelligent than donkeys, horses, oxen, camels and other beasts of burden; they are bigger and stronger than any other land animal and they live in complex social structures in the wild. To make matters worse, very few working African elephants are born in captivity – most individuals were born wild and free, and being removed from their natural lives has impacted on them heavily.

In order for humans to be able to sit safely on an elephant, walk with it or use it for working tasks, the elephant must perform on command, repeatedly and reliably. With an animal so large, even non-aggressive natural movements and actions can result in humans being seriously injured or even killed. Total control, leading to absolute compliance and obedience, is critical. This complete control can only be achieved by dominance and discipline, which nearly always involves 'breaking' the elephant. There are various ways in which a human, generally weighing less than 100 kilograms, can control an intelligent wild animal weighing 4–7 tonnes, but in the end, whatever the control method, the result must be domination.

Domination and total obedience are achieved by both physical and psychological means, including fear, deprivation (food, water, sleep and rewards), confinement and isolation, negative reinforcement, positive reinforcement, restraint, force and violence. Elephants have to be taught that obedience and compliance results in positive consequences such as words of encouragement and food rewards, whereas disobedience will result in negative consequences. Although positive reinforcement (rewards) are used, training for free contact nearly always involves restraint, negative reinforcement and strict discipline, which inevitably leads to cruel practices.

Domination and control need to be regularly reinforced and maintained. In cases where punishment is used to achieve this, the elephant will often become fearful, aggressive and chronically stressed. The continued requirement for obedience and submission can mean repeated punishment, involving pain and stress, and this can lead to a build-up of resentment. The end result can be that the elephant rampages and possibly causes damage to equipment and property, and injury or death to handlers.

In the words of a leading elephant trainer, 'In the latter stages of elephant training, it is pretty much based on a "treat and reward" basis, but the initial stages of training are messy, noisy and not without risk of injury, sometimes fatal, to either elephant or trainer.'

The various pieces of equipment used by trainers are:

- The hook (or bull hook, known as the 'Ankush' in Asia) is a pole just over a metre (3½/4 feet) long, and 7–8 centimetres (3 inches) in diameter, with a hook and a point at the thicker end, and a metal head at the other.
- Long pole – this is about 3 metres (10 feet) long, and about 13 centimetres (5/5½ inches) in diameter. In some cases a 10-centimetre (4-inch) blade is attached to the end of the pole, in other cases, a metal ball.
- Short stick – similar in dimensions to the 'hook', but without a hook at one end.
- Chains and ropes of various types and sizes are used in training, both as a means of forcing the animals to do things, and as restraints.
- Electric prods – these devices are sometimes known as 'hotshots' and deliver powerful electric shocks.

The equipment mentioned is not necessarily in use in South Africa, and is not necessarily used by all trainers. There are good and bad trainers; some will be deliberately cruel to get results, and others will have more patience and rely to a greater degree on positive reinforcement.

Bully and his fellow Kruger orphans were never 'trained' as such by John Brooker and Old Joe. They were adopted as orphans and grew up in a system of routines to which they became accustomed. The Glen Afric elephant grooms sometimes carried ordinary sticks, and padded chains were used for restraint. The elephants weren't trained because there was no reason to train them to respond on demand to specific commands. If called, they came, simply because they had been used to being rewarded for obedience since they were babies.

On Glen Afric all they had to do was be elephants, albeit elephants that shared their lives with humans. Glen Afric's elephants are rarely used for filming anymore, are never transported for filming, and Jenny Brooker insists that nowadays they are never required to do anything that isn't natural and voluntary.

Very few working African elephants are born in captivity.

Wandering in 750 hectares and occasionally being filmed is in stark contrast to being required to perform on command.

Bully has been much luckier than Duna; he has never been trained to do anything he didn't want to do. The nearest he has come to this was being offered inducements like the orange-coated Nokia phone. In contrast, Duna had a violent brush with training that left him badly damaged psychologically. They are now both lucky to enjoy a life of near total freedom at Inverdoorn. They are very much the exceptions: most captive elephants are not so lucky and will live in closely restrained captivity for the rest of their lives.

'Our elephants are ambassadors highlighting issues facing wildlife, conservation, and conservationists in an ever changing, modernising, and less than ideal world.' Sean Hensman

Rory Hensman is widely acknowledged as having been one of the best elephant trainers in Africa. He died in 2013 but he is survived by his wife Lindie, and his children Sean, Michael and Mary. It was to Rory and Lindie Hensman that Clem Coetzee had sent Mishak to learn how to train elephants. Mishak is quite clear that, although chains and ropes were at times used by the Hensmans for restraint, he never saw any deliberate cruelty. The elephants were trained slowly, and training speed was dictated by the response of each individual animal. Mishak is adamant that provided he is given time, he can train elephants to accept human riders and perform other tasks without having to use training aides such as poles, chains, ropes and negative reinforcement.

Rory's son Sean makes the same claim about training elephants to accept human riders: 'It's a slow process, it's exactly the same as when you train a horse. No behaviour that is trained is behaviour that an animal can't perform. An elephant going down, or an elephant lifting a leg, are things they perform naturally in the wild. An elephant flying is not natural and you can beat or try to coerce them till they are black and blue but you will never get one to fly!'

He continues, 'Every behaviour that is trained, is actually a natural behaviour anyway. Training is very simple, there are a million ways to skin a cat. To get an elephant to go down you can beat it, you can stretch it, or you can have a parallel bar a metre above the ground and then hold food underneath it. This encourages the elephant to go down to get the food and once it goes down you give him his reward. Back in the day no one knew how to do it except by force but we've learnt. It's like Monty Roberts with his horses; in the old days breaking a horse involved breaking its spirit using violence, then it would never put a foot wrong in its life. That was then; now we've learnt and guys like Monty Roberts have shown there are many other ways to do it.'

Hensman also believes that, because of their intelligence, a part of elephant training can be allowing them to watch other elephants performing tasks; this way, they quickly pick things up and imitate what they see the trained animals doing. He tells the story of when they were doing research that needed an elephant to exhale into a device so they could catch some of its breath. The elephant they had selected refused to do it. They started working with the elephant in the next pen, which was happy to perform the task and got the consequent rewards and praise. They then returned to the first elephant, which now exhaled into the breathalyser with enthusiasm; he had learnt by copying his friend and was eager for reward and praise.

Hensman explained further: 'Animals will compete for attention and for food rewards and this helps training. Seeing other animals has a calming effect; if you have a docile old bull who is used to the training system, and a young elephant arrives to be trained, the older animal can have a very powerful calming and reassuring effect, which can really assist with training. I guess it's like going to boarding school; the new boy very quickly learns from the experienced older pupils.'

According to Sean Hensman, in 2014 there were 125 trained elephants in South Africa.

He claims that wild elephants are taking food out of the hands of his trainers within three or four days. He acknowledges it varies from animal to animal, but generally they are walking up and down corridors within two or three weeks, and within four or five months the trainers are touching their backs. Lindie and Sean Hensman believe that successful non-violent training of elephants is based on trust between trainers and elephants, and that training the trainers is more difficult than – and as important as – training the elephants.

According to Sean Hensman, there is no organisation in South Africa that monitors the training of elephants or tries to ensure that owners adopt best practice methods. However, Dr Marion Garai did start the Elephant Managers & Owners Association (EMOA) (subsequently closed), and other organisations were also started, notably the Elephant Trainers Association (ETA) and the Elephant Managers Association (EMA). Hensman regrets that the associations never worked effectively enough, and puts this down to competition between owners, and their not wishing to share trade secrets.

According to Hensman there are 125 trained elephants in South Africa. In addition, there are elephants living on small private game reserves in varying degrees of captivity, which takes the total captive population to between 150 and 200.

A visit to YouTube on the Internet reveals a wide selection of films showing elephants being horrifically abused in training. Elephants being trained for circus performances in the USA, and for working in Southeast Asia, are shown being violently abused by trainers. There are good and bad practitioners in all areas of human activity, but it's probably fair to say that in the past, using violence and cruelty to train elephants was the norm. Today, most Western countries have laws that forbid cruelty to animals, and trainers largely try to avoid outlawed methods when training their animals. Nevertheless, it would be naive to think the practice has died out altogether, as is evidenced on YouTube.

No matter how benign the training regime, the morality of keeping elephants in captivity, and of making them work, must be questioned, and in general terms the answer can only be that it is wrong.

'Tusk actively supported the 1989 CITES ban on the trade in ivory, and since then the charity's position has not changed. Tusk remains firmly against the re-opening of any legal trade in ivory from whatever source. There are too many uncertainties, and the risks to elephant populations are too great.'

TUSK

# 17

# THE AFRICAN ELEPHANT TODAY

he futures of two of Africa's largest mammals are in serious doubt. In 2014 in South Africa alone 1,215* rhinos were poached, and it is estimated that one elephant is being killed by poachers every 15 minutes. This ongoing killing spree is driven by the increasing demand for rhino horn and elephant tusks. The demand comes almost exclusively from Southeast Asia and China, where mistaken medical beliefs and the desire for ivory and horn trinkets, baubles and ornaments is pushing both of these African icons towards extinction in the wild.

It is thought that in the 1930s there were between three and five million elephants living wild throughout much of Africa – the figure most often quoted is 3.5 million. By the late 1970s, numbers had more than halved to 1.3 million, then by 1989 the figure had halved again to 600,000. Wild elephants are found in up to 38 African states, but 70 percent are located in only seven countries – Botswana, Kenya, Namibia, South Africa, Tanzania, Zambia and Zimbabwe. Will Travers of the Born Free Foundation remembers the Director of Wildlife of the Central African Republic (CAR) telling him in the 1970s that that country had 70,000 elephants; today there are fewer than 1,000 elephants in the CAR.

Travers believes that the total number of wild elephants in the whole of Africa is now less than 400,000, a number that would yield an annual birth rate of around 20,000. There are many different estimates of exactly how many elephants are being poached each year, but even the lowest figure is higher than Travers' estimate of the birth rate.

The three main reasons for the collapse in numbers are ivory poaching, habitat loss and fragmentation, and human-wildlife conflict (HWC). Of the three, poaching is by far the greatest threat; and the world watches in helpless frustration as each year the value of horn and ivory increases, along with the number of poached animals, and their corresponding slide to extinction in the wild.

In 2012 the IUCN African Elephant Specialist Group (AESG) estimated numbers to be as in the table below. It must be remembered that all figures are estimates as elephants don't stand still to be counted, are often in cover, and are migratory; and census techniques may differ. Figures from some sources are for all elephants, including those in private game reserves and parks, whereas others apply only to wild populations. As a result, figures may sometimes appear to disagree, but there is no disagreement as to the threat posed by ivory poaching.

## STATUS OF ELEPHANTS – 2012

| Region | Definite | Probable | Possible | Speculative |
|---|---|---|---|---|
| Central Africa | 16,486 | 65,104 | 26,310 | 45,738 |
| Eastern Africa | 130,859 | 12,966 | 16,700 | 7,566 |
| Southern Africa | 267,966 | 22,442 | 22,691 | 49,057 |
| West Africa | 7,107 | 942 | 938 | 3,019 |
| Totals | 433,999 | 89,873 | 54,636 | 105,380 |

Note: That the figures don't add up may be a reflection of the difficulty in producing precise numbers.

There are a few places, notably Botswana and South Africa, where elephant numbers are increasing. In places like Chobe in Botswana, and the Kruger and Addo parks in South Africa, increasing numbers are a cause for concern, and population control is being considered.

Sceptics argue that, unless ivory poaching is stopped, it is only a matter of time before it reaches these places, and population control becomes irrelevant.

As usual, money is the driver. Together with drugs, human trafficking, and arms, the trade in wildlife and animal parts is now among the top four illegal global trades. These trades all have the world's intelligence agencies and police forces deployed against them, and yet each year trafficking increases in value and volume. In Africa this translates into more dead elephants and rhinos, and richer corrupt officials. Illegal wildlife trafficking is not a worldwide problem in the same way as the trade in drugs, arms and humans because, in the case of wildlife, demand comes mostly from one distinct area, and supply is restricted to another. This should make it an easier proposition for governments and law enforcement agencies to tackle.

It is often argued that, whether it's shark fins, pangolins, ivory or rhino horn, if demand from China and Southeast Asia were shut down, then the problem would disappear. If wildlife is a global resource, and illegal trading a global problem, then why is it not being dealt with more effectively by treaty at the United Nations, with states who break the treaty having meaningful sanctions applied against them? The answers are that there's a lack of political will, and that despite the impression given by the headlines in Western media, wildlife is a low priority.

In 1987 the price of raw, unworked ivory was $5 per kilogram; by 2010 it was $150, and in 2014 in China the wholesale price for raw ivory was $2,100 per kilogram. These figures show the dramatic increase in the value of ivory, and while the poachers only receive a

In a few places like Chobe in Botswana, and the Kruger and Addo parks in South Africa, the increase in elephant numbers is a cause for concern.

fraction of this money, for poor African families struggling with the day-to-day realities of survival, it is more than enough to tempt them into poaching. They then serve the interests of crime syndicates and in some cases, ultimately, even terrorist organisations, e.g. al Shabaab. For the traffickers, businessmen and crime syndicates, ivory is nothing more than another profitable product – but with an ever increasing demand and value.

An argument common to the trades in rhino horn and ivory is that controlled legal sale of these commodities would reduce or eliminate poaching by undermining profits, and hence preclude the need for an illegal supply. There are strong and persuasive arguments on both sides of this debate, but the facts below sway the debate in favour of no trade at all.

1. If the value is high enough, and the demand is strong and increasing, then legal and illegal trades can thrive side by side.
2. Keeping and guarding stockpiles needs a large financial investment that often uses up limited resources in countries where the money would be better spent on conservation measures.
3. Increasing supply often merely increases demand, and reducing the price simply makes the commodity affordable by more people. This helps lead to the situation referred to in point 1.
4. Legal supply of a commodity often serves as a way to launder illegal stocks.
5. The side-by-side existence of legal and illegal supplies sends mixed messages and leads to confusion, and can create law enforcement difficulties differentiating one from the other.
6. A controlled legal supply could only be administered by efficient, well resourced state organisations that are free from corruption. Sadly, corruption is so entrenched in many African countries that the ability to administer and police controlled supplies would be compromised.

On 19 July, 1989, Kenya burnt its 12-tonne ivory stockpile. In the years since there have been several such symbolic burns and in January 2014, Chinese authorities destroyed more than 6 tonnes of certificated ivory. 'No trade' leads to legally held stockpiles, which can be a temptation to reintroduce trade in the future; but some experts argue that destruction is wrong because it means the animals have died in vain, and a valuable resource is being lost, which could be used for conservation. Both points are valid, but the second option needs an efficient, corruption-free system to ensure that money raised from stockpile sales gets to the right places. Sadly, as mentioned in point no. 6, there are currently no guarantees in this regard.

No one country can solve a global problem and, although China, Thailand, Japan and other Southeast Asian countries constitute most of the demand, ivory can also be found in many places in Europe, the United States and elsewhere. The only way to end ivory poaching is to kill the demand, and that should be simple, shouldn't it? Ban sales, make all domestic and international trade illegal, destroy stocks, and hey presto – problem solved! This looks good until you consider the trade in drugs, where these measures are already in place to a large extent, and still the drugs war is being lost. The conclusion has to be that part of eliminating demand must be increasing awareness and education. Research has shown that most consumers of ivory and rhino horn don't realise they are pushing these species towards extinction, that most of the supply is illegal, and that cruel and painful death is involved.

In most countries with a demand for these wildlife commodities there is state education, state-run radio and TV, agencies with websites, and social media capabilities. Therefore, their governments possess the instruments needed for fast, effective awareness and education; that relatively little is happening brings us back to political will and priorities.

The TV-watching armchair conservationist sitting in Europe or the United States has a very different view of elephants from that of the rural African whose daily life can be threatened or otherwise affected by them. Many rural African populations fear elephants, and suffer as a result of the destruction they cause, and so have a deeply ingrained hostility towards them.

It is easy to want to save elephants if you live in London or New York and are unaffected by them; however, if they have killed one of your relatives, or wiped out your maize patch and left your family starving, you are likely to have a very different view! Although human-wildlife conflict (HWC) involves many humans and many

animals all over the world, it is often at its most acute in Africa; and elephants are one of the species that most often come into conflict with humans. The answer to resolving HWC is to ensure that rural populations see a benefit in living alongside elephants; without such a guarantee, they will never entirely support their conservation.

Time is running out for us to solve these issues or we will be living in a world without wild African elephants: unthinkable, yes – impossible, no.

THE QUESTION IS,
ARE WE HAPPY TO SUPPOSE THAT OUR
GRANDCHILDREN
—— MAY NEVER BE ABLE TO SEE ——
AN ELEPHANT
EXCEPT IN A PICTURE BOOK?

NATURE
PBS.ORG/NATURE

~ Sir David Attenborough

*Culling is only one of several options available to those managing elephant numbers.*

# 18
# POPULATION
# MANAGEMENT

The African elephant is under pressure in every way. As we saw in the last chapter, in some areas like the Kruger National Park, Addo Elephant National Park and Chobe National Park, increasing numbers are causing concern, and the need for population control is an ongoing issue. In other areas, poaching is taking a dreadful toll, making the need for population control measures irrelevant. Where poaching is rife, survival – not population control – is the key issue.

The three factors that control elephant populations in the wild are natural mortality, predation and environmental conditions. In closed areas like game parks, all three of these natural control mechanisms are likely to be compromised to varying degrees.

There are very few areas remaining in Africa that are large enough to be considered viable, stand-alone, properly functioning ecosystems in which elephants can roam. Most elephants live in parks and reserves that are of a specific size and often delimited by fences. No matter how large, these areas are rarely fully functioning ecosystems and a degree of human management is required. In the late 1980s and early 1990s the elephant-carrying capacity of the Kruger Park was thought to be in the region of 7,000 animals. Culling was used to regulate numbers until 1995, when it was abandoned as a population control method. Culling is a controversial and highly emotive subject, and opinion is polarised on both sides of the argument. In 2008 South Africa announced that small, strictly regulated, scientifically based culls could recommence. However, no further culls have yet taken place in the Kruger Park, or on other government-controlled land.

Culling is only one of several options available to those managing elephant numbers.

Translocation is the physical transporting of elephants from one area to another. As a means of population management it has obvious limitations. It can only be used with relatively small numbers, so would help very little in relieving pressure in an area like the Kruger National Park. For a while, juveniles were transported to less populous areas, but this was of only limited and short-term benefit; and when the young translocated elephants grew to sexual maturity, they reproduced and caused the same problem in their new homes.

Another concern with translocation is that, unless whole families are moved together, there can be negative impacts on social structures within herds and family groups. For example, in the Pilanesberg Game Reserve mature bulls had to be introduced to 'educate' juvenile bulls.

Hunting can provide valuable revenue, but this needs to be managed in such a way that it benefits local communities whose lives are affected by the presence of elephants; such revenue can help mitigate against the negative impact of human-wildlife conflict (HWC). However, as a population-control measure it has very limited effect: majestic, but older animals that have stopped breeding are often targeted by hunters, and numbers of elephants individually hunted are low. Hunting can also traumatise survivors and make them frightened and wary of humans, and this can lead to aggressive behaviour.

Contraception is being successfully used on elephants and many other mammals, in particular a brand of immunocontraception called Porcine zona pellucida (PZP). The vaccine is administered by darts; with smaller herds vehicles are used, while larger herds are usually treated from helicopters. Each dose of PZP costs about $35, which breaks down to $11 for the delivery system (dart) and $24 for the dose. For many reasons, PZP is an attractive alternative to culling. It is 100 percent effective and the dose affects only the sperm receiver; this means that if males are darted by mistake, there are no adverse behavioural side effects. Females can be darted regularly and remain unable to conceive. Unlike culling and hunting, contraception does not produce an adverse public reaction.

However, although it was initially thought there were no adverse physiological side effects, there is now published data showing that PZP can have negative impacts on elephants. One of the concerns is that, by limiting or eliminating the production of babies, managers are interfering with the way elephant society works, and this could have various negative effects, including making breeding-age females depressed. In addition, contraception is more expensive than culling; and, when treating large herds, unless treated animals can be identified, it is inevitable that many will be darted more than once, leading to even greater costs.

What is certain is that there are no simple, one-size-fits-all answers. Translocation may work for small numbers; many believe that properly managed hunting can play a limited role; contraception ticks most of the boxes; and culling will remain a dirty word and a highly emotive subject.

A question that has to be considered in the context of the story of Bully and Induna is whether the policy of sparing the babies was right or whether, in hindsight, the babies should have died with their families.

Being spared, and reared by humans, kept the orphans alive, but we must question what sort of lives they have led, deprived of growing up in a natural, wild, elephant family: there were no

**171**

mothers, matriarchs, siblings, other relatives or herd bulls to teach them elephant ways and language. Their natural life in a herd with social structures was taken from them and would never be able to be fully replaced. Their freedom will forever be limited.

Bully, Duna, Three, Hannah and Marty are among the lucky ones: they are not required to perform, have large areas in which to roam, and are allowed to be real elephants, doing their own thing. Many of the Kruger orphans have ended up in zoos, and Duna and Gambo were both seriously and cruelly abused. Unless they are in a reserve or park large enough to have a herd or whole family group, no captive elephants are living completely natural lives, and as a result many will have serious behavioural problems.

It can be argued that an elephant born in captivity knows no other life, so doesn't understand it is in captivity; but do elephants that have been captured and removed from the wild know they have been condemned to a life of imprisonment? With animals this intelligent, there is at least a chance that some of them won't forget what they once had, and know what they are missing.

In the years since Bully lost his family, our knowledge of elephants has increased enormously. The question that must haunt those who spared elephant babies in the 1980s culls is whether life is always preferable to death. When it involves the loss of living a natural, wild life, and the risk of enduring physical and psychological damage, the answer for most people is – with hindsight – probably a resounding no!

It can be argued that an elephant born in captivity knows no other life.

# EPILOGUE

# ELEPHANTS NEVER FORGET

ully seemed to know exactly where the sun would appear over the faraway hills in the Tankwa Karoo. He raised his trunk and saluted the birth of a new day. Soon Mishak would arrive and give them breakfast, and then Bully would push open the steel door of the boma and lead Duna out into a day of foraging, mud and dust bathing, playing and surveying his domain. It would be a normal day on the Inverdoorn Game Reserve as Bully and Duna enjoyed their freedom ... or would it?

As Bully was saluting the sunrise, Jenny and Jonathan Brooker were getting into their car at their holiday home outside Cape Town, and Jenny set the satnav to direct them to Inverdoorn.

Jonathan was excited and nervous. He had been looking forward to this day for four and a half years. He had promised Bully he would find him and see him again, and today he would keep his promise. The excitement was almost too much, but underlying it was doubt and fear. Would Bully recognise him, or would his old friend have forgotten him, bringing his dreams crashing to earth?

Jenny was enjoying the drive to Inverdoorn, but she understood why Jonathan was so quiet and why the usual incessant stream of questions had dried up. Christo, the head ranger, was waiting for them, and after introductions and refreshments, Jonathan was on his way to his moment of truth.

Mishak was sitting in his vehicle about 100 metres from Bully and Duna, watching Christo and the Brookers approach. He knew the purpose of Jonathan's visit and understood that Bully's reaction wasn't just important to Jonathan today; it would stay with him for the rest of his life.

Mishak told Jonathan to stand by the vehicle and he walked towards Bully and called him. If Bully could feel the intense expectation in the air he didn't show it. His steps were hardly giant ones as he sauntered slowly towards Mishak. Jonathan watched his friend drawing nearer and his heart beat faster with each step. Bully reached where Mishak was standing and raised his trunk and flapped his ears as if to ask why he had been called. Mishak turned and beckoned, and Jonathan wasn't sure if he wanted to run to Bully or whether nervousness had turned his feet to lead.

'Hello Bully, I've missed you, I told you I would come and find

'Hello Bully ...

you.' There was a deep rumble, and Bully first raised his trunk, then slowly moved it to Jonathan and touched the side of his face. Tears welled up in Jonathan's eyes and rolled down his cheeks. 'I knew you would remember me, I knew you would.'

Mishak kept an eye on Duna, but he needn't have worried – Bully had clearly transmitted his calm and happiness to Duna who stood close by and watched the reunion.

Nearly a box of fruit and an hour later and it was time for Jonathan and Jenny to go. Jenny had also said hello to Bully and he had very obviously remembered her too. Jonathan leant his face against Bully's and whispered goodbye, and very gently Bully raised his trunk and touched Jonathan's face. Then he turned and climbed up the bank onto the track and walked off.

Watching him moving away down the track, both Jonathan and Jenny had tears in their eyes. Bully had proved that elephants don't forget. He looked happy, calm and content. Bully finally had the home he deserved.

*I've missed you.'*

Jenny also said hello to Bully.

Jonathan leant his face against
Bully's and whispered goodbye.

# ACRONYMS

| | | |
|---|---|---|
| AERU | – | African Elephant Research Unit |
| AESG | – | African Elephant Specialist Group (IUCN) |
| CAR | – | Central African Republic |
| CITES | – | Convention on International Trade in Endangered Species of Wild Fauna & Flora |
| EMOA | – | Elephant Managers & Owners Association |
| ETA | – | Elephant Trainers Association |
| HWC | – | Human-wildlife conflict |
| IUCN | – | International Union for the Conservation of Nature |
| PMMA | – | Para-Methoxymethamphetamine |
| PZP | – | Porcine zona pellucida |
| SANParks | – | South African National Parks |

Sometimes they are used for scratching or playing, but trees are easily pushed over.

# USEFUL WEBSITES

Born Free Foundation – www.bornfree.org.uk

CITES – www.cites.org

The David Sheldrick Wildlife Trust – www.sheldrickwildlifetrust.org

Elephants for Africa – www.elephantsforafrica.org

The Endangered Wildlife Trust – www.ewt.org.za

Inverdoorn – www.inverdoorn.com

Knysna Elephant Park – www.knysnaelephantpark.co.za

Save The Elephants – www.savetheelephants.org

Space For Giants – www.spaceforgiants.org

TRAFFIC (the wildlife trade monitoring network) – www.traffic.org

Tusk Trust – www.tusk.org

WildAid – www.wildaid.org

Working Wild – www.wildcareafrica.blogspot.com

World Wildlife Fund – www.wwf.org

From birth, baby elephants start
being educated by their elders.